ISO 9000
Family of Standards
with extracts from ISO 9001 Audit Trail (First Edition)

ISO 9000
Family of Standards
with extracts from ISO 9001 Audit Trail (First Edition)

David John Seear

authorHOUSE®

AuthorHouse™
1663 Liberty Drive
Bloomington, IN 47403
www.authorhouse.com
Phone: 1-800-839-8640

Published by AuthorHouse   09/06/2012

ISBN: 978-1-4772-2640-7 (sc)
ISBN: 978-1-4772-2641-4 (e)

Any people depicted in stock imagery provided by Thinkstock are models, and such images are being used for illustrative purposes only.
Certain stock imagery © Thinkstock.

This book is printed on acid-free paper.

Because of the dynamic nature of the Internet, any web addresses or links contained in this book may have changed since publication and may no longer be valid. The views expressed in this work are solely those of the author and do not necessarily reflect the views of the publisher, and the publisher hereby disclaims any responsibility for them.

INDEX

QUICK TIP:—

Knowing how busy people are I recommend that for a quick read concentrate on the BOLD TEXT only and you will quickly pick up the messages within the book. Then if you require more detailed information please read the adjacent text.

1.0 Introduction

There is a considerable difference of opinion as to what the ISO 9000 Family of Standards (FoS) consists of and how the documents should be used.

They are a set of generic standards of immense benefit to business because they can help any organisation to manage, control, and improve their business. Most organisations are aware of ISO 9001 however there is a lot of misunderstanding about how ISO 9001 should be used and many companies do not even have ISO 9000 or know about ISO 9004. It should be noted that ISO 9000, 9001 and 9004 are a set of standards that are able to support any types of organisation. Unfortunately not many Organisations are aware of the benefits hence the reason for this document.

This book is an attempt to help Organisations choose the standards that are most applicable to their business from the ISO 9000 Family of Standards (FoS)

2.0 Scope

The scope of this document is identified in ISO 9000 where it defines the ISO 9000 Family of Standards (FoS) as:—

ISO 9000 Quality management systems—Fundamentals and vocabulary

This describes the fundamentals and specifies the terminology for quality management systems.

ISO 9001 Quality management systems requirements

This specifies requirements for a quality management system where an organisation needs to demonstrate its ability to provide products that not only fulfil customer and applicable regulatory requirements but also enhances customer satisfaction.

ISO 9004 Managing for the sustained success of an organisation—A quality management approach

This provides guidelines that consider both the effectiveness and efficiency of the quality management system. The aim of this standard is improvement in the performance of the organisation and increased satisfaction of customers and other interested parties.

ISO 19011 Guidelines for auditing management systems

This strictly speaking is a support document applicable to organisations that carry out audits of management systems. It focuses, in particular, upon the competence of those involved in carring out audits and how they control and manage this activity.

Note 1:—Authors comment: ISO 19011, although identified as part of the family, it is in fact a document that guides auditors, organisations and certification bodies in the correct control and application of auditing. In its latest issue 2011 it has gone from guidance on environmental and quality audits (2002) to cover a much broader range of auditing activity (2011).

Note 2:—It is not the intention of this document to go through all the relevant clauses in each standard but to take samples to help illustrate the purpose of each standard.

Note 3:—The purpose of this book is to make interested parties aware of how to use the ISO 9001 Family of Standards and hopefully **improve the standard of auditing**.

3.0 Summary

There are just four documents in the ISO 9000 Family of Standards (FoS) and each has a different purpose. It is the author's opinion that not fully understanding the purpose and roles of the ISO 9000 (FoS) is the principal reason why ISO 9001, the most commonly used standard, is often misunderstood.

ISO 9000 sets the ground rules and covers the terminology that should be used. It has a pivotal role within the four standards and it is designed to support the other three documents within the family to help any type of organisation manage its business in the most effective manner. It covers the eight management principles developed from the "Vision 2000" findings. It includes the basic fundamentals of a quality management system including the common terms and definitions used in quality.

ISO 9000 is the "backbone" to the "Family of Standards". As such it is important that each standard in the Family should, in their section "Normative References", refer to ISO 9000 as being an applicable reference.

ISO 9001 has a restrictive role, it enables an organisation to demonstrate its ability to consistently provide products that meets customer needs and applicable statutory and regulatory requirements. It covers agreeing with the customer what they require (Specification), then ensuring the process is planned and managed to ensure those requirements will be met. It should be noted that the statutory and regulatory requirements are only those that relate to that **product** and it is not every statutory and regulatory requirement that an Organisation has to deal with. There are many misunderstandings about ISO 9001 and some of these are covered in this book.

In many cases auditors are still being taught to see if the organisations management system has covered all the clauses 4-8 in ISO 9001. This stems from what was called the Document Review where an organisation's Quality Manual is examined to see if it has recognised and addressed all the requirements of ISO 9001 in principle. This "desktop" stage 1 audit is a specific training element from a Lead Auditor Course. It should be recognised that the Quality Manual is just a stated intent nothing more. It is a commitment explaining "WHAT" an Organisation does. It does not have to cover Why, When, How, Where and Who. The true situation is only revealed, at the levels below the Quality Manual, when a professional **process audit** is carried out to ascertain if the processes that have been put in place can consistently achieve the specified requirements. **How can an auditor ascertain if the process is able to consistently meet the specified requirements if they do not know what the specification for the product is?**

ISO 9001 has a restrictive purpose and that is to ensure that the Organisation has a management system that can consistently meet the customer's requirements. It is restricted to the process from enquiry through to delivery of the product. Certification to ISO 9001 is intended to give the Customer confidence that the management system employed by the Organisation can be relied upon to consistently meet the specified requirements.

ISO 9004 is the standard that covers the other requirements that an Organisation has to manage, that have not been addressed by the ISO 9001 standard. It includes "Risk and Strategy" and the whole purpose of ISO 9004, as stated in the title, is managing for the sustained success of an organisation. In other words it covers all the issues outside the scope of ISO 9001 that could affect an organisation's ability to be successful. This is why the whole ISO 9000 Family of Standards (FoS) should be taught, not just ISO 9001.

ISO 9004 is the final part of the Trilogy of standards that enables any Organisation to address the broader quality management issues relating to the sustained success of their business. Where ISO 9001 finishes ISO 9004 fills the gap as it provides a much wider focus on quality management than ISO 9001.

Finally ISO 19011 are the guidelines for auditing management systems. This was previously just for quality and environmental management systems (2002) but the new ISO 19011 (2011) is generic and suitable for many of the other management system standards that have been published. This standard gives guidance to the auditing activities related to management systems. It emphasises the need to conduct process audits, yet this is still misunderstood in many quarters.

ISO 19011:2011 actually illustrates how things can go wrong when standards are expanded to include other issues. ISO 19011 attempts to cover a much broader range of auditing. In doing this, the original purpose has been lost. This is illustrated by the fact that it states that no Normative References are cited. In other words ISO 9000 is no longer applicable. In this statement alone it has excluded itself from the ISO 9000 Family of Standards.

The four standards (FoS) are all explained with specific examples of how and where they may be utilised and gives organisations an opportunity to decide what stage they are at and which of the four standards are most applicable to their business.

The book itself is an attempt to identify how the ISO 9000 Family of standards should be used. It identifies some examples of incorrect use and common mistakes made in the interpretation of these standards, in particular ISO 9001. As the author does not wish to imply criticism of what is an excellent Family of Standards he has identified a 5 Year Improvement Plan that could help quality regain credibility by using the standards correctly. (See Appendix C) Revising a standard on the grounds of improvement when the standards are not used correctly is counterproductive.

The approach taken with ISO 19011 gives concern over the approach that could be taken over the ISO 9000 and ISO 9001 revision due 2014? This continual drive to add issues that should reside in ISO 9004 into ISO 9001 will, if implemented, undermine the whole ISO 9000 Family of Standards and is one of the reasons for this book.

I don't expect all readers to agree with all the views in this book, however, I would request that this book is read with an "Open Mind" leaving preconceived views to one side. I will leave the reader to decide if any of the views and proposals within this document could or should be implemented.

4.0 ISO 9000

4.1 Introduction

This standard, as stated in its title, covers the fundamentals and vocabulary.

Let us look at what this means:—

First of all in the introduction 0.1 it confirms that the ISO 9000 Family of Standards includes just four standards. (See section 2 Scope above)

KEY 1 The ISO 9000 Family of Standards (FoS) consists of ISO 9000, ISO 9001, ISO 9004 and ISO 19011.

It goes on to identify the 8 management principles that were identified by a committee set up to investigate the weaknesses of ISO 9001 in the early 1990's. They reported back to the ISO TC/176 committee in around 1993. At that time TC/176 felt this was too big a change to be included in the 1994 version of ISO 9001 as many other countries were starting to use ISO 9001. It was therefore felt that it was NOT the time to make a radical change. Following the decision not to introduce the committee's findings until the following issue it became known as "Vision 2000".

This meant that the "Vision 2000" findings formed the basis of the "Step Change" in the ISO 9001 standard where they identified the importance of:—

EIGHT MANAGEMENT PRINCIPLES

a) Customer focus
b) Leadership
c) Involvement of people
d) Process approach
e) System approach to management
f) Continual improvement

g) Factual approach to decision making
h) Mutually beneficial supplier relationships.

The above eight management principles formed the basis for the quality management system and should be considered whenever the ISO 9000 (FoS) are being used. (See ISO 9000 for detailed explanation)

KEY 2 The eight management principles should be referred to when interpreting what is required within the ISO 9000 Family of Standards (FoS).

The interesting thing came about when the link to "Plan Do Check Act" (PDCA) was introduced into the structure of ISO 9001 2000.

Figure 1 Plan Do Check Act

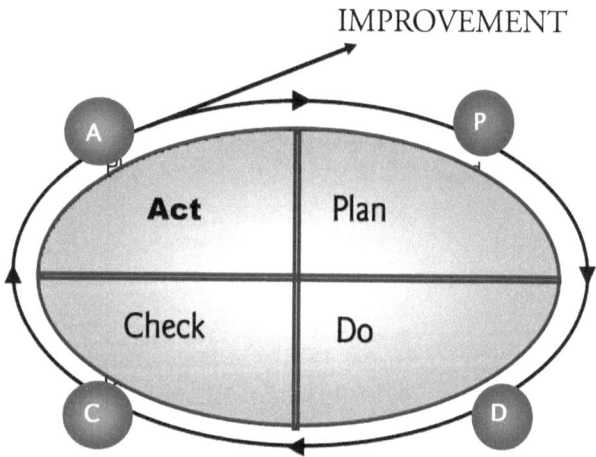

The "ACT" above should leads to an improvment

If you look at ISO 9000 Figure 1—Model of a process based quality management system the central wheel in that figure covers "Resource Management", "Product Realisation", "Measurement Analysis and Improvement" finishing with "Management Responsibility". As can be seen this mirrors the PDCA approach.

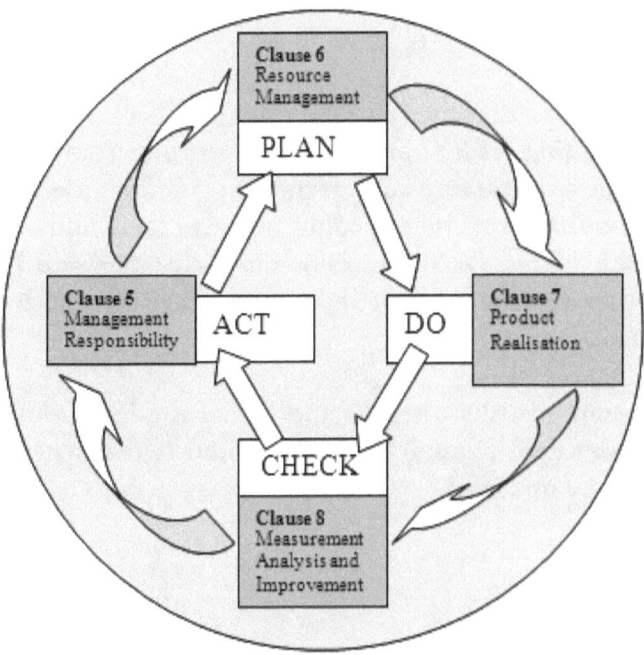

Figure 2 Relationship between Plan, Do, Check Act and ISO 9001

Plan	Resource Management
Do	Product Realisation
Check	Measurement Analysis and Improvement
Act	Management Responsibility

The "Act" above leads to an improvement

This PDCA approach was chosen in order that the eight management principles could be implemented within a defined structure. This location of the individual clauses within ISO 9001 has been known to cause dissent in quality discussions as some parts of Measurement Analyses and Improvement should, in some peoples view, be in Product Realisation. When however the model in figure 1 of ISO 9000 is explained, including the link to PDCA, they are able to see the logic behind why the individual ISO 9001 clauses have been introduced in the manner they have. The logic behind the ISO 9001 structure is then normally accepted.

It is such a shame that the full ISO 9000 (FoS) are not introduced at the beginning of an organisations introduction to quality management as well as into auditor training. If they understood how all the parts fitted together it could improve their understanding of how each of the (FoS) compliments each other and helps an Organisation manage, control and improve their approach to their quality management system.

KEY 3 Training in the purpose and use of the ISO 9000 Family of Standards (FoS) should be implemented if the benefit of the Family is to be obtained.

4.2 Scope

The ISO 9000 standard itself is well worth examining in detail as it covers many of the basic principles that should be understood before getting involved with the other standards within the ISO 9000 (FoS). This is especially true of ISO 9001 because these two standards should be considered a matched pair. In other words don't use one without detailed knowledge of the other.

ISO 9000 itself covers the benefits that an organisation can obtain through implementing a quality management system. It highlights a mutual understanding of the terminology used in quality management, including suppliers, customers and regulators so that there is less chance of misunderstandings. It also forms the "Backbone" to the numerous quality related standards that are often termed Guidance Documents". (See Appendix A)

4.3 Fundamentals of a quality management system (QMS)

ISO 9000 explains the rationale for using a quality management systems and how important it is to meet customer expectations. It is therefore essential to understand the customer's requirements. To do this requires the organisation to analyse customer requirements, define processes that contribute to the achievement of a product that meets those requirements.

It highlights the difference between requirements for quality management systems and those for products. It emphasis that the quality management system requirements are specified in ISO 9001 and are generic and applicable to organisations in any industry or economic sector regardless of the offered product category. Within the fundamentals of quality management systems it highlights the importance of Systems Approach and Process Approach both identified in the Eight Management Principles. The introduction concludes with Quality Policy and Objectives and how important it is as it provides focus and direction for the organisation.

It covers the value of documentation where it enables communication of intent and consistency of action. It achieves repeatability, helps with training and allows objective evidence to be judged against the documented requirements. This in turn ensures the effectiveness and the continued suitability of the Quality Management System (QMS) to be evaluated against the defined criteria.

KEY 4 Organisations should understand the value of documentation where it is needed to enable communication of intent and consistency of action

It clearly shows a model of the process-based QMS.

It highlights the role of "Top Management" as this was a major concern picked up by the "Vision 2000" team. It was found that the failure, under the older versions of the standard, to clearly define the role of top management within their QMS and how the processes worked was a major problem undermining the credibility of using a QMS. In many cases organisations were appointing a Quality Manager then carrying on as they had in the past. It was as if "Quality" was something different and had a life of its own. This was perpetuated by the manner in which quality was explained.

This is why "Leadership" in the eight management principles received a high profile within the requirements. ISO 9000 explains that through leadership and actions top management can create an environment where people are fully involved and in which a QMS can operate effectively. It even highlights the eight management principles from the introduction as something that can be used by top management as the basis for their role.

KEY 5 The quality management system (QMS) is the organizations management system and does not have a separate life of its own.

It is not unusual to see quality, environment, health and safety shown as totally separate activities as if they have a life of their own. Even the document control of these systems may be different and this does not help.

It is not the intention of this document to repeat what is in this section but it does cover the role of top management with nine different things (ISO 9000 Clause 2.6) that they should be dealing with.

It is hoped that on reading the above there will be a demand by Organisations to obtain a copy of ISO 9000 2005. I can assure any manager that if their Organisation is ISO 9001 Certified and they don't have and understand ISO 9000 2005 they will not be able to comply with ISO 9001 2008 requirements.

ISO 9000 covers the auditing and review of the QMS.

- It defines the first party audit as an internal audit.
- It defines a second party audit as an audit conducted by the organisation on their suppliers either directly or by other persons appointed by them.
- It defines third party audits as audits carried out by external independent organisations. Such organisations are usually accredited to provide certification services.

Once again this is a brief summary.

It also emphasises the importance of management reviews. This is identified as regular systematic review of the organisations activities and results referenced against the QMS or model of excellence. It highlights the importance of self assessment stating that it provides an overall view of performance of the organisation.

KEY 6 Management review is the opportunity to gather information and make decisions on how to improve the Organisations processes and activities.

Then we get to Continual Improvement. The aim of continual improvement of a QMS is to increase the probability of enhancing customer satisfaction. It should be recognised that ISO 9000 is relevant to all the other standards within the ISO 9000 (FoS).

It also covers the role of statistics within an organisation. These are linked directly to the importance of information that facilitates better use of available data to assist in the decision making process. This in turn links to one of the eight management principles "Factual approach to decision making".

The above is just a summary of what is in ISO 9000 before it gets on to Terms and Definitions. It does however set the scene for how it should be used.

4.4 Definitions

Terms and definitions are a major part of ISO 9000.

My own experience is that despite this being an International Standard and the importance of having a common understanding of the terms used in quality, even experienced quality professionals do not have a common understanding of what these terms mean.

This section on definitions is broken down into ten different sub headings:—

They are terms relating to:—

- Quality
- Management
- Organisation
- Process and product
- Characteristics
- Conformity
- Documentation
- Examination
- Audit
- Quality management or measurement activities.

It should be noted that the alphabetical index at the back of the ISO 9000 standard is the best place to check to see what definitions have been defined.

Let me give the reader a few examples of where Quality professionals often get things wrong. Let us look at a couple of common errors.

Anyone who has read my earlier book on "Audit Trail;" will recognise the importance of carrying out process audits following an Audit Trail. Unfortunately Audit Trail has not been defined in ISO 9000. It is still hoped that this will be included in the next edition of ISO 9000. Audit Trail was first formally raised in December 2009 and was published in IRCA Inform issue 24 and the ISO 9001 Auditing Practices Group (APG) at the same time. (App B). There is plenty of individual support but no formal recognition that there is a commitment by the ISO committee TC 176 to consider this, despite the fact that Audit Trail is a requirement in international auditor education.

(See www.pdqms.co.uk where two definitions have been defined. Inform Issue 24 and APG Audit Trail) This is also in the Audit Trail extracts at the back of this book.

The two definitions below are ones that I have made a mistake with on more than one occasion because I did not cross refer to the definitions in ISO 9000.

What is the difference between Audit Plan and Audit Programme?

Audit Plan

Description of the activities and arrangements for an **Audit (3.9.1)**

Audit Programme

Set of one or more Audits (3.9.1) planned for a specific time frame and directed towards a specific purpose.

In the past I have submitted an Audit Plan and called it an Audit Programme. It is easily done. However we as quality professionals should take a leaf out of our own book and ensure we use the correct terminology.

Let us look at other frequently misused terms:—.

What is the difference between Audit Finding and Audit Evidence?

Many people believe that audit finding is what you found. This is incorrect

Audit finding is defined as results of the evaluation of the collected **audit evidence (3.9.4)** against **audit criteria (3.9.3)**

As you can see the Audit Finding is the evaluation of the audit evidence against specific criteria.

Audit evidence is defined as **Records (3.7.6),** statements of fact or other **information (3.7.1)** which are relevant to the **audit criteria (3.9.3)** and verifiable.

Then we get to **Audit conclusions**

Outcome of an **audit (3.9.1)** provided by the a**udit team (3.9.10)** after consideration of the audit objectives and all **audit findings (3.9.5)**

In plain English, Audit Evidence leads to Audit Findings which in turn leads to Audit Conclusions.

ISO 9000 is the home for the more generic terms used in Quality. There is a drive to bring other unrelated terms into ISO 9000 such as "Stakeholder" As you will see later this term actually belongs in ISO 9004.

KEY 7 Introducing other terms to ISO 9000, such as "Stakeholder", when there already is a term for "Interested Parties" should not be contemplated. The term Stakeholder should go into the standard to which it is relevant, which is ISO 9004.

The other issue is that there is no definition for "Audit Trail" which does belong in ISO 9000. Unless you carry out a Process Audit following an Audit Trail it is impossible to comply with the scope of ISO 9001. The scope states that ISO 9001 specifies requirements for a quality management system where an Organisation needs to demonstrate its ability to consistently provide product that meets customer and applicable statutory and regulatory requirements.

It is not possible to do this unless the Organisation or the auditors identify the requirements, take selective samples and audit the process following an Audit Trail to see if the process is able to consistently meet the specified requirements.

Both IRCA Inform Issue 24 and ISO 9001 Auditing Practices Group recognised this and published an article by the Author on the 10th December 2009. So far "Audit Trail" has not been formally introduced into the ISO 9000 family of standards. However, there is a requirement in IRCA Auditor courses to follow an Audit Trail.

It has been stated that ISO 9001 APG was just advisory and had no power. The outcome being this was not even discussed at the TC176 committee despite the promise by senior personnel that it would be.

I have no more to say on definitions except to note there are eighty four (84) definitions defined in ISO 9000 and I would like to think that we, as Quality professionals, use them correctly. This cannot be done if over 70% of Quality Professionals do not have access to ISO 9000:2005.

KEY 8 ISO 9000 should be in every Quality Professional's tool kit or how else will Quality Professionals talk the same language?

It is also important to recognise that other Quality related standards, may quite correctly, define definitions in section 3 of that specific standard, however all the ISO 9000 (FoS) should refer to ISO 9000 as a Normative Reference in section 2. Failure to do this undermines the Family concept.

KEY 9 ISO 9001, 9004 and ISO 19011 should all state, in section 2.0 of each standard, that ISO 9000 is a Normative Reference or how could they be considered part of the same Family of Standards (FoS).

ISO 9000 Annex A

After the definitions there are informative annexes.

A1 Introduction

Explains the methodology used in the development of the vocabulary. It highlights that the universal application of the ISO 9000 (FoS) requires the use of a technical description but without the use of technical language and a coherent and harmonised vocabulary that is easy to understand by all potential users of quality management system standards.

A2 Content of a vocabulary entry and the substitution rule.

This covers the concept of variants within a language. E.g. American English and British English. The old statement the USA and the UK are separated by a common language still holds true today.

It even explains how this should be dealt with in some detail.

I have heard people state that in a particular country they don't have that word. I always use the example of Taxi. Many people did not have the word Taxi but it was soon picked up and used in many different countries and it became a common word in their language. The same goes for the word Computer which is now used world wide.

A3 Concept relationships and their graphical representation

In terminology work, the relationship between concepts is based on a hierarchical approach considering all the inherent characteristics of the concept. It gives many different relationships such as, concepts relating to management, concepts relating to organisation, concepts relating to process and product and are generally used to assist anyone who is dealing with the structure of definitions and how they can be put together.

This explains how and why the 10 different headings were used and how the decision was made regarding which heading any individual definition would reside under.

Bibliography

It finishes with Bibliography relating to relevant standards that were cross-referenced in the development of ISO 9000.

I hope from the above simple summary the importance of ISO 9000 will be recognised and all Quality professionals will make sure they have access to it. It is after all the "Backbone" to the ISO 9000 (FoS) and is used to understand many other Quality related standards and documents. Without it we cannot possibly achieve the intended outcome.

<u>Figure 3 Current ISO 9000 Family of Standards (FoS)</u>

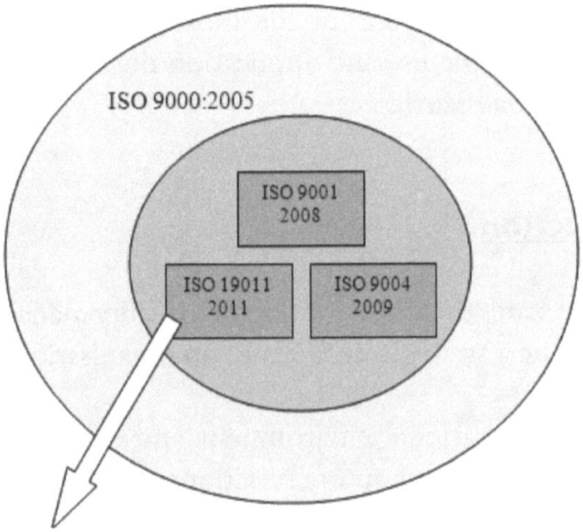

Appendix A?

> **Note 1 ISO 9000 should be a Normative Reference to all standards in the ISO 9000 Family of Standards (FoS)**

> **Note 2 ISO 9000 may also be identified as a Normative Reference by any other quality related standard (See Appendix A)**

The failure to reference ISO 9000 in the Normative References of ISO 19011:2011 is likely to require its removal from the ISO 9000 Family of Standards. This would leave the ISO 9000 Family of standards as ISO 9000, ISO 9001 and ISO 9004.

ISO 19011 could easily reside with other support documents (See Appendix A).

5.0 ISO 9001 Quality Management System – Introduction

General

If we judge the success of a standard by the number of copies issued then ISO 9001 must be one of the most successful of all the ISO standards. However the use and application does not have a common understanding for all parties.

5.1 Introduction

This is where it states that the adoption of a quality management system (QMS) should be a strategic decision of an organisation.

It covers the organisational environment and any changes and risks associated with it. It covers an organisations varying needs, objectives, the product it provides, the processes it employs and the size and organisational structure.

It goes on to state that it is NOT the intent of this standard to imply uniformity in the structure of an organisations QMS or its documentation.

ISO 9001 confirms that it can be used by, both internal and external parties including certification bodies to assess the organisational ability to meet customer, statutory and regulatory requirements applicable to the product and the organisations own requirements. (It is not possible to comply with the Scope of ISO 9001 if the management system is only written to just meet the requirements of clauses 4-8 of ISO 9001).

KEY 10 The Statutory and regulatory requirements, as far as ISO 9001 is concerned, are only those statutory and regulatory requirements that relate directly to the product.

Note:-ISO 9001clause 3 indicates that wherever the term "Product" occurs, it can also mean "Service"

It also indicates that the quality management principles stated in ISO 9000 and ISO 9004 have been taken into account during the development of this standard. Once again this confirms the link between these three standards. There is no mention of ISO 19011 and that is why despite ISO 9000 indicating that ISO 19011 is part of the family in truth the ISO 9000 (FoS) is really just ISO 9000, ISO 9001 and ISO 9004.

ISO 19011 is important to the success of the other three and it may seem logical to include this standard however the drive by other parties to increase the ISO 9000 family beyond these four standards should not be countenanced as this could complicate and confuse the issue. (See Appendix A for related standards that are **NOT** part of the ISO 9000 (FoS)

KEY 11 The ISO 9000 Family of Standards (FoS) should NOT be extended beyond the current four standards of ISO 9000, ISO 9001, ISO 9004 and ISO 19011.

Process Approach

The next significant issue is the promotion of the Process Approach this was, to anyone involved in auditing to earlier versions of the standard prior to certification, well known. In fact no effective audit could be carried out without auditing the process following an Audit Trail. Unfortunately the rush to qualify enough people to do third party audits led to some basic auditing skills being missed. In fact many training organisations only taught people to audit to see if the ISO 9001 clauses 4-8 were covered in the organisations management system. They missed the true purpose of auditing namely to ascertain if the process being used achieves what it should achieve.

For an Organisation to function effectively it has to determine and manage the numerous linked activities. The process approach enables the activities to be a transformation of inputs into outputs.

$$INPUT \longrightarrow ACTIVITY \longrightarrow OUTPUT$$

KEY 12 All audits should be process audits following an audit trail or it is not possible to verify if a process is effective in meeting the required output.

To understand a process it is sometimes useful technique for the auditor to draw a simple flow chart/process map of the process (See example next page)

The advantage of the process approach is the ongoing control that it provides over the linkage between the individual processes within the system of processes.

In this section it clearly references the methodology known as Plan, Do, Check, Act (PDCA) already mentioned in the section on ISO 9000.

It is explained as

Plan
Establish the objectives and processes necessary to deliver the results in accordance with the requirements and the organisations policies.

Do
Implement the process

Check
Monitor and measure processes and product against policies, objectives and requirements of the product and report the results

Act
Take actions to continually improve process performance.

Below the "Note" on PDCA is the Figure 1 of ISO 9001 covering the model of a process-based quality management system. As already stated in section 4.0 of this document covering ISO 9000 the PDCA directly relates to section 5, 6, 7, and 8 of ISO 9001 and is the reason the ISO 9001 is structured in this manner. Section 4 covers the quality management system that controls all of these four areas. We must not forget section 1-3 as they are paramount to understanding the purpose, scope, limitation and controls applicable to using the standard.

Simple Car Servicing Process Map

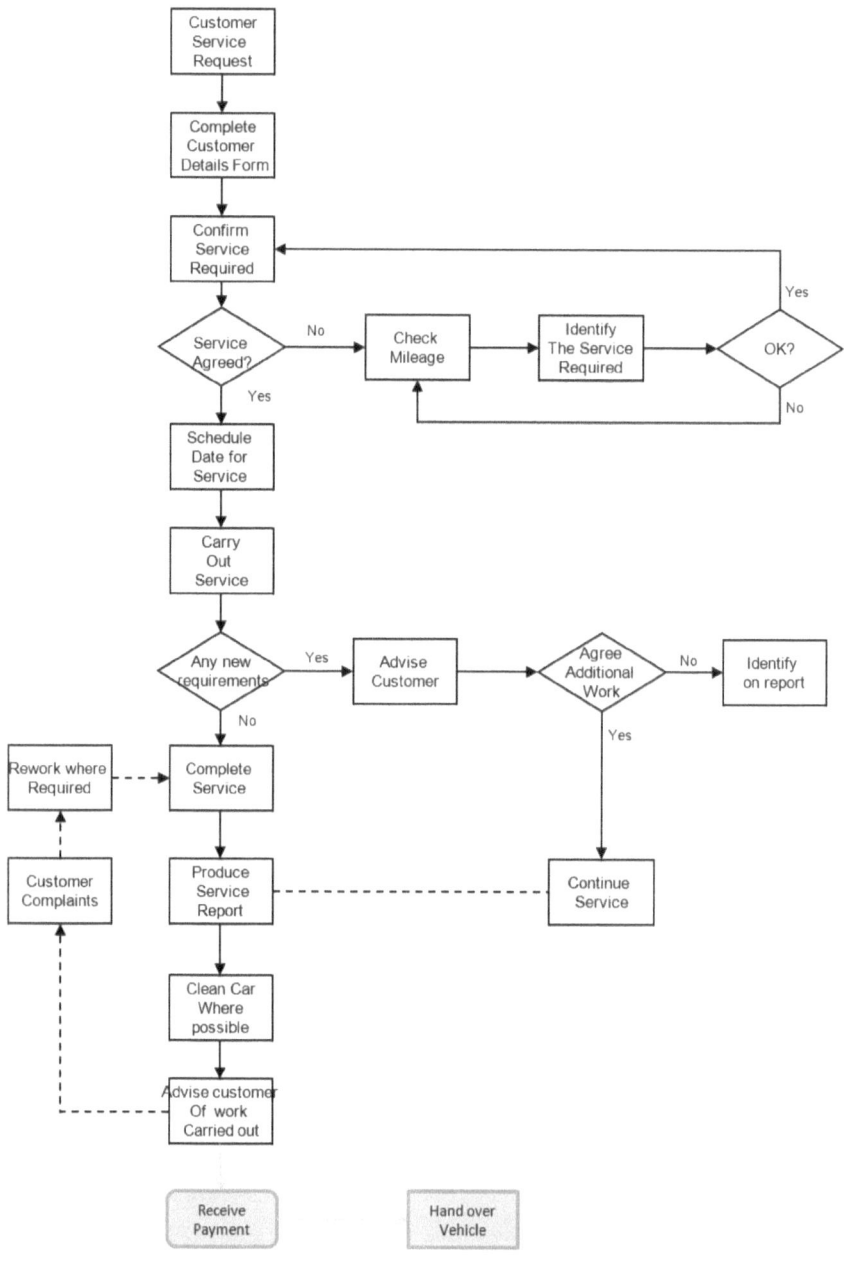

Relationship with ISO 9004

It states that ISO 9001 and ISO 9004 are quality management system standards that have been designed to **complement** each other, **BUT** can also be used independently.

ISO 9001 specifies requirements for a QMS that can be used for internal application by organisations, or for certification, or for contractual purposes. It would however be strange to use ISO 9001 or ISO 9004 in isolation without cross-referencing to ISO 9000, as mentioned in clause 2 Normative References.

It focuses on the effectiveness of the QMS meeting the customer requirements.

Note:—as you will see later ISO 9004 is not a standard that an Organisation can be certified to.

KEY 13 The ISO 9001 standard restricts its scope to the management system that directly relates to meeting the customer and applicable statutory and regulatory requirements.

ISO 9004 provides a wider focus on quality management than ISO 9001 and is designed to provide guidance to management for achieving sustained success for any organisation in a demanding and ever changing environment.

It concludes with the statement that ISO 9001 does not include requirements specific to other management systems, such as those particular to environment, occupational health and safety, finance management or risk management. (Introduction 0.4)

KEY 14 The ISO 9001 standard does NOT include other management systems such as, Environmental, Occupational Health and Safety, Finance and Risk Management.

Compatibility with other management systems

It concludes with compatibility with other management systems

Where it explains that during the development of ISO 9001 due consideration was given to the provision of ISO 14001:2004 to enhance the compatibility of the two standards for the benefit of the user community. It also highlights Annex A in ISO 9001 which shows the correspondence between ISO 9001: 2008 and ISO 14001:2004.

We now move on to the purpose and scope of ISO 9001.

It should be noted that all the comments to date are in the Introduction of ISO 9001 and as such they are not part of the Quality management system requirements covered by ISO 9001 certification. Please do not misunderstand this statement the actual ISO 9001 for certification purposes starts from Quality Management Systems—Requirements section 1 Scope starting from Page 1, however as you can see you should not ignore the ISO 9001 introduction.

5.2 ISO 9001 Quality Management Systems—requirements

It should be noted that when carrying out certification audits all eight main clauses of ISO 9001 should be considered not just the clauses 4-8 as this is incorrect. There are many people who seem to think that the audit is to see if the organisation has a management system that covers clauses 4-8. This is also incorrect. I do not exaggerate when I say that 50% of audits do not achieve the basic purpose and scope as specified by ISO 9001.

This is where sections 1-3 of ISO 9001 are absolutely essential if the scope of the standard is to be complied with. (See below)

Clause 1.0 Scope

General 1.1

ISO 9001 specifies requirements for a Quality Management System where an organisation:—

a) Needs to demonstrate its ability to consistently provide product that meets customer and applicable statutory and regulatory requirements, and

b) Aims to enhance customer satisfaction through the effective application of the system, including processes for continual improvement of the system and the assurance of conformity to customer and applicable statutory and regulatory requirements.

The above are quite simple and explicit however due to misunderstandings the approach taken by some organisations to fulfil these requirements does not meet either of these basic requirements.

Let us look at what they mean and compare that with what currently takes place.

Before we do that there are couple of notes below clause 1.1:—

Note 1 The product itself only applies to what is intended for or required by the customer. It also states it is any intended output resulting from the product realisation process. (ISO 9001 Introduction Figure 1)

This is again very clear. **It indicates the primary process is that achieved by product realisation.** Bringing in any other issue is not valid. In simple terms it is agreeing what the customer requires, planning how this will be achieved then doing it and providing the product as per contract or order to the customer.

Note 2 States Statutory and Regulatory requirements can be expressed in legal terms.

So let us look at what is meant by Statutory and Regulatory requirements.

There are people of some stature in the quality world who believe it is all the Statutory and Regulatory requirements relevant to the Organisations business. This is wrong as the only **statutory and regulatory requirements are those that directly relate to the product itself.**

The above interpretation of Statutory and Regulatory requirements has caused many people a lot of concern as they have not been taught this. In fact I have been asked by many quality professionals to justify my view.

My reply was as follows:—

ISO 9001 Scope covers the organizations ability to consistently provide product that meets customer and applicable statutory and regulatory requirements.

Clause 1.1 General Note 1 indicates the product only applies to the product intended for or required by the customer or to any intended output resulting from the product realization process.

Clause 3 The term "product" can also mean "service"

Logic dictates as the Product is all that the scope of ISO 9001 covers then the statutory and regulatory requirements are also only those requirements that directly relate to the product that is provided to the customer.

This means that if the product itself is not constrained or required to meet any statutory and regulatory requirements then they are not relevant to ISO 9001.

Let us look at application (1.2)

It clearly states that ISO 9001 is a generic standard and intended to be applicable to all organisations regardless of type, size and the product provided.

It also indicates that only clauses within section 7 product realisation can be excluded provided such exclusions do not affect the organisation's ability, or responsibility, to provide products that meets customer and applicable Statutory and Regulatory requirements.

A classic example is where there is no material provided by the customer then 7.5.4 Customer Property can be excluded. It also means that if there is nothing brought in that is used in the product or service provided to the customer then even Purchasing 7.4 can be excluded. When auditors are advised that purchasing is not applicable they state "but you do buy things" the organisation states they do and quite often the auditor indicates that purchasing is applicable. Once again this is wrong.

This leads me back to the auditing of a process following an audit trail. **If purchasing is not applicable this will be evident when auditing the process as there is nothing in the process that is bought in. This confirms that the purchasing process is not relevant to the product being provided to the customer against the requirements of ISO 9001. This should highlight the importance of auditing the process.**

In fact in many cases the organisation just gives in and lets the auditor audit their purchasing department despite the fact there is nothing in that department that affects the product they provide. It is this failure to understand the true purpose of ISO 9001 that is the problem.

Note:—It is important to understand that what is being discussed is the restrictive purpose of ISO 9001 and in particular the scope of certification. There is not one Organisation that having used ISO 9001 for Certification would not choose to use the tools provided within that standard to help them with all other areas of their business. The concern is that some Certification Bodies go beyond their role and try to take ISO 9001 Certification into the wider business activities. That would be fine if Certification did in fact ensure that organisations could consistently provide product that meets the specified requirements. Unfortunately that is not being achieved and the reason is the type of audit carried out does not

audit the process following an Audit Trail. (Auditing clauses 4-8 to see if they are mentioned in the management system is, as already stated, not effective)

Another amusing situation is where an organisation claims to do design. When they are challenged about this and asked what they design they state their quality management system. Once again this is **NOT** part of the product that is provided to the customer and is therefore not relevant.

KEY 15 Remember ISO 9001 clause 1.1 Note 1, The term product only applies to product intended for, or required by a customer or any intended output resulting from the product realisation processes.

All l can hope is that you get the gist of what is being said.

KEY 16 The key processes for product/service delivery is section 7 Product Realisation with, as required, able support from the other clauses.

Clause 2 Normative References

We are now at Normative references where it states that ISO 9000 2005 is <u>indispensable</u> for the application of this document. It has a dated version of ISO 9000 so that only ISO 9000 2005 is applicable.

Surely the fact that ISO 9001 indicates that ISO 9000:2005 is **<u>indispensable</u>** would mean that all ISO 9001 Certified organisations would be aware of and possibly have a copy? A survey carried out indicated that 70% of ISO 9001 Certified organisations were not. It is this poor understanding of how the ISO 9000 (FoS) helps and supports each other that highlighted the need for a book like this. Yes you can rely on a consultant however even some consultants and certification bodies have not fully understood how ISO 9000, ISO 9001 and ISO 9004 form a coherent set of quality management system standards to help any organisation manage their business.

The final part in the first three sections is

Clause 3.0 Terms and Definitions

This is where it states that the terms and definitions given in ISO 9000 apply.

Also included in the previous version namely ISO 9001:2000 was:—

SUPPLIER ——→ ORGANISATION ——→ CUSTOMER

This was removed in the 2008 version and I find it hard to understand why as it helps people with the terminology that should be used. The Organisation is your company, the supplier is the organisation that supplies you and this supply can be through a purchase order or by contract. The customer is the person you supply.

All the above is in the first page of ISO 9001 where it covers the first three clauses. The sad thing is in many cases these ISO 9001 page 1 fundamentals are ignored.

AUTHORS NOTE:—

I recognise that many quality professionals may not, initially accept my view on ISO 9001 as this is not what they have been taught, however all I ask is that you keep an open mind on comments that have been made. Particularly auditors as I would ask each of you to judge if your type of audit is able to judge if the organisation can consistently achieve the required output from the process being audited?

This cannot be done if you do not take the time to find out what the intended output should be.

Clause 4 Quality Management Systems.

General requirements

This section covers how you develop, control and manage the system that you have put in place. It requires the organisation to determine: the processes needed and their application, the sequence and interaction, the controls and criteria used to judge that they are in control and how they decide which resources are needed to ensure the processes are adequate and in control. This includes Human Resources, Infrastructure and the Work Environment.

The whole of ISO 9001 is like a "Checklist" that enables the organisation and/or the auditor to judge if the Management System is adequate to ensure that the process will consistently meet the agreed requirements.

It covers establishing the documents required, such as Quality Policy, Quality Objectives, Quality Manual. It also highlights that although the standard only requires six documented procedures the organisation should include any other documented procedures, work instructions etc needed to run the business. It also covers the fact that you need to keep records and implement the controls that are necessary. It should be noted there are many records required as mentioned in various clauses of ISO 9001. There is a clause on Records 4.2.4 that gives clear guidance on what should be considered when keeping records.

All the above is just good common sense and over the decades of running IRCA registered auditor courses I have never had anyone say that a requirement in ISO 9001 is nonsense. I have however had many organisations say that their quality Management System is bureaucratic. They indicate that they have had to put in many more procedures. I always explain that it is up to them, using ISO 9001 and its clauses, including mandatory requirements to decide what is appropriate for their organisation. There are many instances when procedures and other documents have been forced upon an organisation by their Consultant, Auditor or Certification Body.

A question I often ask on my courses is:—

Is it possible to audit a department where there are no documented procedures or instructions?

Normally the majority of participants on a course say no. I have to explain that this is wrong you can audit a department but you just have to "walk" through the process following an example so you can understand how it works. Then, taking a selective sample (chosen by you), then use the processes you have been shown to follow the chosen samples through the process. This allows you to see if the process is being followed and does actually achieve the intended output for that process.

The next question is usually what happens if the person gets run over by a bus? How do you ensure the process will be carried out correctly then? My answer is training and competence. There is nothing wrong with having a training document that explains how it all works. It does not have to be a procedure, providing the person is competent and trained in doing what is required for that process. Let us get it clear, the organisation is responsible for deciding what documentation is required. In some cases, because auditors don't seem capable of auditing without a procedure, they indicate that the organisation must write a procedure to cover that process. This is wrong.

KEY 17 The Organisation is responsible for developing a management system that meets their requirements not the Certification Body.

Far too often people indicate they have a procedure yet when you examine it, the document is in reality a training manual. I had one procedure that ran to 135 pages and no one, but no one, understood it or used it.

The old **KIS** technique cannot be beaten. **KEEP IT SIMPLE**. If you have trained competent people do you need a massive amount of documentation? No you do not. The standard itself states that the organisation should ensure that people have what they need to do their job, so don't drown them in paper or computerised documentation systems. Each organisation should itself decide on what is needed to run their business NOT outside bodies.

There are some specific things that must be noted.

a) Outsourcing that affects product conformity to requirements must be controlled. An organisation cannot absolve their responsibility by outsourcing the activity. It requires that the type and extent of control to be applied to these outsourced processes, should be defined within the Quality Management System.

This makes sense as you, the organisation, are always responsible for meeting the customer's requirements. **An interesting question here is do you accept ISO 9001 Certified organisations as sub contractors to you? Do you think the standard of ISO 9001 certification gives you the confidence to outsource something you require on the basis they are an ISO 9001 Certified organisation?**

This is followed up in clause 4.1 Note 1 where it is explained that the process for managing these activities is included in all four sections 5, 6, 7, and 8 of ISO 9001. It should also be noted the same approach applies to all your own management activities.

There are too many individuals who still audit the clauses of ISO 9001 as if they are independent requirements with no relationship at all to any other clause within the standard. This is complete nonsense

EXAMPLE

A recent example of this was Quality Policy where certification auditors and consultants stated that the clause on Quality Policy does not say the policy has to be signed and approved by the Chief Executive Officer. (CEO MD etc). They explained that it did not say that in clause 5.3. It was pointed out that this document had to be managed as any other document in the QMS and would need approval and control covering document identity, issue, date etc. (4.2.3). If you understand the purpose of the Quality Policy there is only one person who can sign and approve it if it is to have credible authority. The easiest way to achieve this is to sign it, however it is up to the organisation to demonstrate that it is controlled and who has the authority to issue it.

It is this continual drive to interpret each clause as if it is a stand alone statement that makes the ISO 9001 standard ineffective. Does the Quality Policy need to be signed? The answer is that it is up to the organisation, however the auditor should ascertain that however it is controlled it is effective.

This leads me back to the importance of the scope and clauses in section 1-3.

All clauses need to be considered by the Organisation, Auditors and Certification Bodies in relationship to the requirements in these first three sections of the ISO 9001 standard. They should not be ignored or skipped over!!

If we do not ensure that each part of the process is robust and can ensure that the process is capable of consistently providing product that meets the specified requirements, then we are not meeting the scope and purpose of the ISO 9001 standard.

EXAMPLE

I was running a lead audit course in the USA and one person raised a non conformity and called up 12 clauses to justify raising the nonconformity.

I advised him that he only needed to identify the most relevant clause.

However, as an exercise we, as a group, went through the clauses that were raised one at a time and they all had a legitimate claim to justify the non-conformity.

Let us face it everywhere you go when doing an audit involves many applicable ISO 9001 clauses e.g.

- Documentation being used.
- Issue number of document is it current?
- What records are kept?
- Responsibility and authority of people doing that job
- Communication that is needed
- Competence of people doing the job
- Infrastructure where the job is being carried out
- Work environment, covering conditions that work is carried out under.
- Actual activity taking place
- Controls in place
- Etc

I could continue however I hope you get the point. You do not audit the clauses you audit the process. The clauses are tools used by the Organisation, Auditors and Certification Bodies to judge if the process consistently meets the specified requirements.

This means that auditors should know what the required outcome of every process should be.

EXAMPLE

Over a decade ago I was carrying out an audit for a certification body and I was asked why I had not put document control on my Audit Plan. I explained that I am looking at document control everywhere I go throughout the audit. I indicated that my reports even highlighted which documents I looked at and what revision number, date etc were being used. I was advised that the accreditation body would not accept this as they insist that document control is given 20-30minutes within the audit plan. It is this poor standard of knowledge throughout the Quality Profession that allows auditing by clauses to be perpetuated.

As a matter of interest when I plan an audit I often ask the organisation to supply their Quality Manual and their Document Control procedure for pre reading especially if it is a product type with which I am unfamiliar. (It also gives me something to read on the plane). This means when I arrive I already understand their processes and how they control their activities.

    b) The term outsourced is explained as a process that needs to be carried out, but the organisation has chosen it to be carried out by an external party.

    c) Outsourcing does not absolve the organisation of the responsibility for conformity to all customer statutory and regulatory requirements.

KEY 18 Outsourcing any activity that could affect the organisations ability to meet the customers requirements does not absolve the Organisation from that responsibility

It also explains that the outsourced process can be influenced by how it would impact on their ability to meet the specified requirements, the degree to which the control and responsibility is shared and the capability of achieving the necessary controls through the application of Purchasing Process.

As already stated the ISO 9001 standard is there to help any organisation in putting in place a Management System that will ensure they meet customer's requirements.

It is important that this is understood. The whole purpose of auditing is to see if the processes being used can consistently meet customer requirements. Auditing by ISO 9001 clause does not achieve this.

There is nothing in clause 4 Quality Management System that should confuse anyone if, and it is a big if, they read the clauses taking into account the Scope, Normative References and Terms and Definitions as stated in ISO 9001 clauses 1-3.

Having a Quality manual is a requirement. The important thing is to understand the purpose of a quality manual. The purpose is simple it allows management to explain to all and sundry "WHAT" they do and what is applicable. It does not have to give any information about how they do it. The manual allows the organisation to identify any exclusions they wish to be exempt from in section 7 Product Realisation (See ISO 9001 1.2 Application) It enables the organisation to identify clauses within the Product Realisation process that are not applicable to the product and can therefore be excluded. It has a link to relevant procedures in the next level down by identify the document number and its title (The issue revision or date are not normally included) It also covers a description of the interaction between the processes of the QMS plus anything else the organisation feels would be beneficial to enable others to understand what they do. It is in fact a very nice sales and marketing tool that can be used for that purpose and enable it to meet ISO 9001 requirements. A lot of organisations include a little history about how long they have been in business and what their products are. Once again a very useful tool in clarifying what the organisation does.

KEY 19. The quality manual is a commitment that explains WHAT the organisation does. It does not have to include the Why, When, How, Where and Who.

Note:—Control of Documents and Records are the first two clauses of the six that require procedures to be written.

Clause 5.0 Management responsibility.

This was one area where there were many problems. Much of this was caused by how Quality management was perceived. In many cases it was seen as a mass of documentation that as far as the organisations management were concerned, did little to help the business. In fact it made running the business more costly and bureaucratic.

Quality management should have been very easily explained. However not many people were capable of explaining the benefit and when Certification became a byword for getting business the Organisations did not always care to find out. The drive was just to keep the certificate and keep the costs down.

The standard tried to address that by applying one of the Vision 2000 management principles namely "Leadership".

Once again these requirements are quite sensible and straightforward. Responsibility and Authority is clearly a sensible thing to define.

EXAMPLE

When at a conference in Iran one of the speakers who ran his own business stated that ISO 9001 allowed him to have holidays. He explained that in the past every expenditure had to be passed to him for approval. Asked if he trusted his managers. he said of course he did, or they would not work for him. When the clause on Responsibility and Authority was explained to him, he realised he could delegate responsibility and give authority for the managers to spend up to a certain amount each week without going to him. At first he received weekly reports with the receipts and totals. When this was seen to be effective he extended it to two weeks. The reason he had initially wanted financial control, was to ensure that he did not have a cash flow problem caused by over expenditure as this could risk the business. He started with a holiday for just one week and was proud to say since implementing ISO 9001 he has had a couple of two weeks holidays every year. He indicated previously he had not had a holiday for years. This meeting in Iran occurred over a decade ago and I hope his holidays are even longer now.

The reason the Management Representative must be one of the management team is to ensure that Quality may be bought up at every management meeting. In this section it covers internal communication and Management Review. The sad thing about this is the current approach to management review is that these meetings are quite often accepted by Certification Bodies as once per year. When you actually talk to Organisations they have many management reviews sometime weekly, monthly or quarterly but they see Quality as nothing to do with the day to day running of the business. It therefore only considered annually.

A QMS does not have a separate life of its own. It is in fact the organisation's management system. This acceptance of annual management reviews by Certification Bodies without judging whether what takes place is effective is another reason why the ISO 9001 standard has lost credibility and had its value diminished.

KEY 20. The ISO 9001 quality management standard has one restrictive purpose and that is to manage the processes controlling the business directly linked to providing the product/service that is capable of consistently meeting the customer's requirements.

Clause 6 Resource Management

This is fundamental to the success of any organisation. It is not just Human Resources but Infrastructure and Work Environment. Once again this is very straight forward however it is often misunderstood particularly the Human Resources. There are Organisations that carry out training audits and only look at the training department. This is another approach where just auditing a specific clause of the standard gives limited benefit.

I have by now hopefully ensured that everyone understands the importance of auditing a process. The only way to audit Human Resources is to link it to an audit of a process taking a note of all the people seen during the audit. Then you choose a sample of the people you have seen going about their duties and then go to the training department to see if the training of these people meets the necessary requirements.

Auditing should not be a "Tick Box" approach by taking each clause within the standard and auditing it because it gives little information and is unlikely to give confidence that the job under review is adequately controlled.

I can't believe I have got to this page without bringing in "Tick Box" auditing as this is the biggest single reason why ISO 9001 is not achieving its purpose.

I will not go through the infrastructure except to say if the buildings, workspace etc are not adequate then the chance of providing a product or service that meets the specified requirements can be compromised.

The same goes for work environment such as noise, temperature, lighting etc as this also can affect the product.

This is where, as explained earlier, ISO 9001 is a tool which allows the organisation as well as the auditor to judge whether the resources that are in place can consistently meet the specified requirements.

My experience is that people do not go to work to do a poor job and, if management give them the tools and the equipment and explain what they want them to do, they will carry out the task in an effective manner. It is after all the management's job to make sure they have competent personnel and suitable facilities.

Clause 7.0 Product realisation

This is where the ISO 9001 action starts. It covers the planning which starts before receiving the order. It is where a decision is made as to whether the Organisation is able to do the specific job and meet the customer's requirements.

It is about planning and developing the processes that would be needed. For an Organisation that makes their standard products this is not such an issue. However for jobs specified by the customer this can be time consuming but beneficial provided the customer and the organisation agree the product specification before starting the work.

Communication

This, like many clauses in ISO 9001, is a brief section however customer communication is a very important issue. There have been many instances where people involved in the job have made decisions without understanding the consequences.

EXAMPLE

The customer was an Oil Company.

An example that comes to mind is when a forged header was required for a bitumen furnace. A call by the supplier to the operations manager stated as they could not meet the delivery for a forged header would he accept a cast header? The operations manager, who was under a lot of pressure to get the plant running, said yes if they meet the time scale. I was actually present when the furnace tubes were being expanded into the header and the header split with a tremendous sound as it cracked in half. All suppliers now know they have to go through the buyer for any change and the buyer knows he has to go back to the requisitioner who in this case was the engineer before any change can be made that affects the product, price, delivery etc.

This is why communication with the customer and those people nominated in this role require a clear understanding of their role and the authority and responsibility they have regarding dealing with the customer.

Once again the inter-relationship between the various clauses in the Standard become evident. **Clauses should NOT be examined in isolation. Any examination should be carried out applying all relevant clauses for that process.**

Design and development (7.3) is fairly straight forward providing the words being used are understood. It is not the intention to go into too much detail in this document except to say all the steps are important including design and development, verification and validation as many people do not understand the difference. It is however made clearer if you read the text carefully. Verification checks if the design and development outputs have met the design and development inputs. Validation is to ensure that the resultant product is able to do what it is supposed to do.

Purchasing (7.4)

Another area where there is a lot of misunderstanding. I will use just one part of the purchasing requirements namely "The Organisation shall evaluate and select suppliers based on their ability to supply product in accordance with the Organisations requirements". This invariably leads the auditor to approved supplier lists. In many cases auditors see the approved suppliers list as demonstrating compliance This approach is totally wrong as it is the auditors role to investigate how this list was developed. Is that process effective and do they have information that allows the auditor to judge that the process used in obtaining an Approved Supplier List (ASL) list does give confidence? Too many times the actual criteria used is the "Lowest Price" and we all know what happens when this is the only real criteria used to make a decision. The current "Tick Box" approach that indicates they have an ASL tells the auditor nothing. The whole purpose of this sentence is simple. If you are buying something then the supplier providing the product should be able to consistently meet your specified requirements. Your Organisations role is to make the requirements clear and unambiguous and it does not end there. The organisations needs to ensure that the supplier being used is able to meet those specified requirements and how this is achieved is crucial to how successful the purchasing process will be. It is up to your Organisation to ensure those suppliers on your approved list have the ability to deliver the product you require. The Auditors role is to judge if the information on each of the supplier's chosen from the selected sample taken are on the ASL and that the information is valid and effective. It is not just to see if an ASL is in place.

There is no need for this document to explain all the requirements as stated in ISO 9001 as they are quite clear from the text in the Standard.

Production and service provision (7.5)

Once again a very simple but effective set of requirements provided they are interpreted in a manner that helps the organisation provide products to the customer. They are very beneficial.

Control of monitoring and measuring equipment (7.6)

Some amusing interpretation can occur here. I will again remind all users of the scope and purpose of ISO 9001. It is to ensure the organisation can consistently meet the specified requirements. The customer requirements are those that relate to the product or service. It is therefore only concerned with monitoring and measuring equipment that is used in checking that the product or service being provided to the customer meets the specification.

Some people believe anything that is used to measure something needs to be calibrated. This is not correct as far as ISO 9001 is concerned. It is only those monitoring and measuring items that if incorrect could affect the product

EXAMPLE

The funniest situation I am aware of is when someone was using an 18" steel rule to underline statements in an A4 document. The auditor decided that as it was a measuring device it needed to be calibrated. When it was explained that it was only used for drawing a red line on paper the auditor indicated that as it could be used to measure something therefore it needed calibrating. This is once again another example of waste of money, time and effort due to lack of knowledge.

The whole idea of an ISO 9001 audit of the management system is to audit the process to identify how effective it is and how well it is structured and controlled. Something that is not used within the process of producing the product or service is <u>NOT</u> applicable to ISO 9001. It is important that auditors make sensible judgements and do not just use ISO 9001 clauses in isolation without checking they are relevant.

I would again remind everyone to consider the scope and purpose of ISO 9001. To understand the monitoring and measuring equipment clause 7.6 it has to be judged against the purpose and scope of ISO 9001. This means it is all to do with the product. Only when this is understood can a decision be made on whether the equipment in question is subject to clause 7.6 of ISO 9001. This applies to all clauses within the family of standards. Clauses should not be interpreted in isolation.

KEY 21 When using each clause it should be referred back to the ISO 9001 scope if it is to be interpreted correctly.

Clause 8 Measurement, analyses and improvement.

As explained earlier this is the key element in gathering information

This section has the four requirements for a documented procedure.

They are:—

- 8.2.2 Internal Audit
- 8.3 Control of nonconforming product
- 8.5.2 Corrective Action
- 8.5.3 Preventive Action

Note:—any other documented requirements are covered in 4.2.1d)

KEY 22 Information = Meaningful Data (ISO 9000:2005) management review without meaningful data (information) is of no use.

The lack of information is the reason why many poor decisions are made.

In the case of ISO 9001 information is contained in the whole of the Standard not just clauses 4-8. Some of the clauses in section 8 could justifiably be put in section 7 Product Realisation, but as mentioned earlier (PDCA), it was decided to use section 8 as the area where this would be captured.

This section covers all areas where information can be gathered from customer satisfaction, Internal Audit, Monitoring and measuring the processes and the product, the control of non-conforming product and the analysis of the data that is produced. All of this and the detail within the relevant clauses help's an organisation make the most of their Management System. It then leads them to the improvement section 8.5.

Improvement (8.5)

It identifies the need to continually improve what the Organisation does. It covers Corrective Action and Preventative Action. Both of which are often incorrectly used. The acronym CAPA is misleading and does not help the understanding as both these terms are NOT related as far as ISO 9001 is concerned. (See below).

One of the early criticisms of ISO 9001 was that Organisation could just have a system and get ISO 9001 Certified without improving what they did.

The "Vision 2000" group recognised this was a major stumbling block in retaining ISO 9001 credibility and identified the need for Continuous Improvement.

This was formally introduced in ISO 9001 2000.

Lets look at three terms used in Quality:—

Correction. This covers where something that was wrong is put right.

Corrective Action To take action to eliminate the causes of nonconformities in order to prevent recurrence

Preventive Action To determine action to eliminate the causes of potential non conformities.

Note 1:—See ISO 9000:2005 for actual definition

Note 2:—Many people even today think Preventive Action is what occurs when you carry out Corrective Action. This is incorrect.

Individuals who believe that Preventive Action is taken to ensure that the Corrective Action is stopped from happening again are wrong. As can be seen from above Preventive Action is to eliminate **potential** non conformities so if something has already happened then the action taken to get back to the root cause of the problem is **NOT** Preventive Action. The sad thing is because it has been incorrectly taught people are now thinking of replacing Preventive Action with "Risk and Opportunity". Once again two wrongs don't make a right. Risk and Opportunity do not belong in ISO 9001 but in ISO 9004. This book on the ISO 9000 Family of Standards attempts to explain how the four standards that make up the ISO 9000 family support each other.

It is not unusual when carrying out an audit to be challenged on Preventative Action and the simplest response is to ask the individual to read 8.5.2 Corrective Action and 8.5.3 Preventative Action.

Normative Reference

As already explained the ISO 9000 (FoS) needs to be treated as such. Even this basic relationship has been misunderstood during the revision of ISO 19011:2011, see section 7.0 of this document, where ISO 9000 is no longer identified as a Normative Reference (see ISO 19011:2011 Section 2.0). When this type of change is made within the ISO 9000 (FoS) it illustrates that the purpose of the Family is not fully understood. How can the revision of ISO 19011 remove the normative reference to ISO 9000. This was required in the previous issue ISO 19011:2002 and changes of this type undermine the Family as the definitions used between the ISO 9000 (FoS) are able vary from standard to standards. (e.g. See definition for auditor in ISO 19011).

It is important to ensure ISO 9000 is applicable to all the ISO 9000 (FoS). Hopefully removal of this link to ISO 9000 will not occur when the changes to ISO 9001 are introduced in 2014?

WILL THE NORMATIVE REFERENCE TO ISO 9000 IN ISO 9001 BE DROPPED?

If this Normative Reference to ISO 9000 is dropped, as occurred in ISO 19011, then the whole purpose of the ISO 9000 Family is undermined.

The above is just one of many misinterpretations of the ISO 9000 (FoS).

Note:—On a small survey of interested parties on the Chartered Quality Institutes LinkedIn forum only a few indicated that they were aware of the four standards that form the ISO 9000 Family of Standards (FoS). Only two Quality professionals were using all four of the standards on a regular basis.

6.0 ISO 9004:2009 Managing for the sustained success of an Organisation

This is the final third element of the ISO 9000 Family of Standards (FoS) that covers the core wider issues of management within an organisation. As explained before ISO 9001 has a specific limited role that ensure all areas of risk are considered when developing and using a Management System that is designed to ensure that the product or service meets the specified requirements. In other words the purpose of ISO 9001 is to enable an organisation to demonstrate its ability to consistently provide product that meets customer and applicable statutory and regulatory requirements

ISO 9004 now fills the gap left by the restrictive ISO 9001 requirements. ISO 9004 attempts to cover all the other relevant issues that have to be considered if the whole Management System controlling all of the organisation's management activities is to be successful. In other words the final part of the structure designed to help manage the continual success of the organisation.

ISO 9004 is therefore a very broad based and detailed Standard that is able to fill the broader management requirements not covered in ISO 9001.

Let us look at the Introduction.

It states that the sustained success of an organisation is achieved by its ability to meet the needs and expectations of its customers and other interested parties over the long term and in a balanced way. Sustained success can be achieved by the effective management of the organisation, through the awareness of the environment, by learning, and by the appropriate application of either improvements, or innovations, or both. ISO 9004 provides guidance to support the achievement of sustained success for any Organisation in a complex, demanding, and ever changing environment by using a Quality Management approach.

This does set the scene quite well by having a diagram Figure 1 that expands on ISO 9001 figure using a wheel within a wheel.

As we have already discussed ISO 9001 uses the Plan, Do, Check, Act (PDCA) approach. This is illustrated in the middle wheel with:—

Plan **Clause 6 Resource management**
Do **Clause 7 Product realisation**
Check **Clause 8 Measurement analysis and improvement**
Act **Clause 5 Management responsibility**

The outer wheel then has ISO 9004 structure of:—

Clause 4 Managing for the sustained success of an Organisation
Clause 5 Strategy and policy
Clause 6 Resource management (extended)
Clause 7 Process Management
Clause 8 Monitoring measurement and analyses and review
Clause 9 Improvement, innovation and learning

Note:—Please refer to ISO 9004:2009 for the broader issues involved

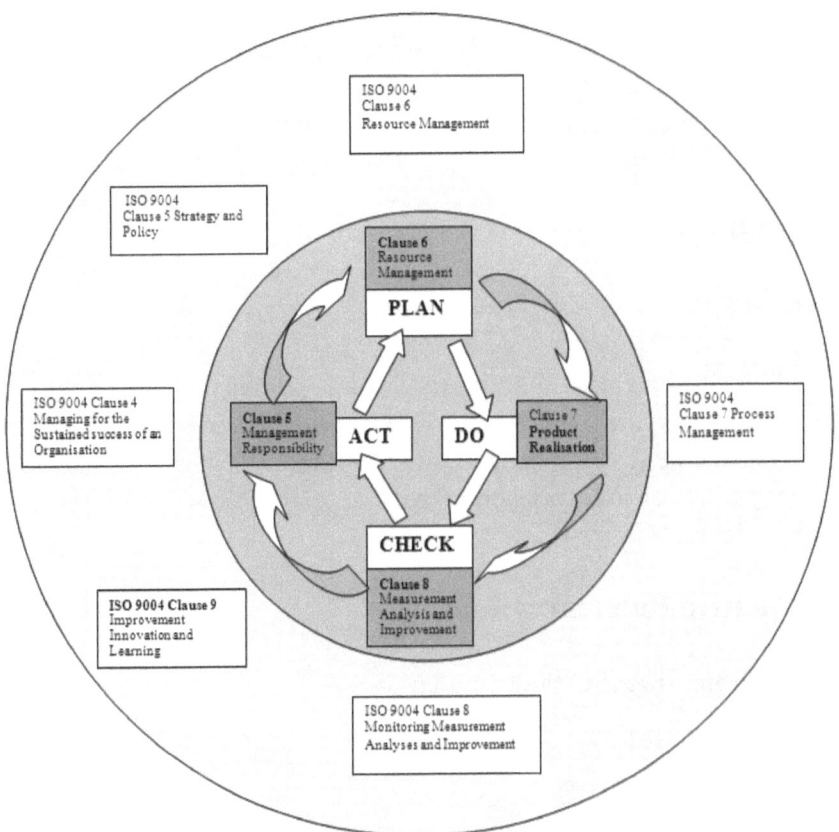

THE LINK BETWEEN PLAN, DO, CHECK, ACT AND ISO 9001 AND ISO 9004

As can be seen ISO 9001 and ISO 9004 clauses 6, 7 and 8 are similar with just slight changes to terminology as it expands the meaning from the ISO 9001 requirements to the ISO 9004 requirements of achieving sustained success over the broader management issues facing any organisation.

Let us look at each ISO 9004 clause one at a time.

There is no intention to cover all or any of the detail as this document is just an awareness document so organisations and Quality professionals can see how the ISO 9000 Family of Standards (FoS) supports each other. It does not and should not be seen as an alternative to the ISO

9000 (FoS); in fact its intention is to make people aware so they actually obtain the ISO 9000 Standards and look at what is being offered.

As I have done throughout this document I will start at the beginning.

ISO 9004

Scope 1.0

This International Standard provides guidance to organisations to support the achievement of **sustained success** by a Quality Management approach. It is applicable to any organisation, regardless of size, type and activity.

Normative References 2.0

Indicates that ISO 9000 applies

Terms and Definitions 3.0

a. The term "Sustained success" is defined
b. The term "Organisation's environment" is defined.
   It is not unusual to have other definitions defined to ensure specific statements within the standard are defined and therefore understood.

Please refer to ISO 9004:2009 for the above definitions. In simple terms sustained success is about achieving the organisations objectives in the long term. ISO 9001 is only about consistently meeting each customer's requirements.

Note:—Section 3 is where the term "Stakeholder", if it is required, should reside providing it is applicable to ISO 9004. I would suggest that if it is required the definition gives a clear detailed statement on who the stakeholders are.

Managing for the sustained success of an organisation 4.0

This mentions **Annex A** Self Assessment where there is information regarding the importance of identifying improvement and innovation opportunities using the self-assessment tools that are provided. As explained this document is intended to give you sufficient information to decide if you should take your knowledge that step further. It will not cover all the elements in ISO 9004:2009 as the Standard does that very well and should be referred to.

The Standard itself is very detailed and helps organisations understand the issues that are involved in the sustained success of an organisation. It allows management to do an assessment of their organisation by giving them the tools to look at where they stand in regard to sustained success.

It also refers to the eight management principles **Annex B** in a little more detail. As you can see the eight Management Principles are what the ISO 9000 (FoS) has been built upon.

B1. General

Is a general introduction that once again references the eight management principles already discussed earlier under "Vision 2000". It states that these principles form the basis for the Quality Management standards prepared by ISO/TC 176 and leads to:—

B2 Principle 1: Customer Focus

This is fundamental principle as Organisations depend on their customers and therefore should understand current and future customer needs, should meet customer requirements and strive to exceed customer expectations.

B3 Principle 2:—Leadership

Leaders establish unity of purpose and direction of the Organisation. They should create and maintain the internal environment in which people can become fully involved in achieving the organisations objectives.

B4 Principle 3:—Involvement of people

People at all levels are the essence of an Organisation and their involvement enables their abilities to be used for the organisations benefit.

B5 Principle 4:—Process approach

A desired result is achieved more efficiently when activities and related resources are managed as a process.

B6 Principle 5 System approach to management

Identifying, understanding and managing interrelated processes as a system contributes to the organisations effectiveness and efficiency in achieving its objectives.

B7 Principle 6 Continual improvement

Continual improvement of the organisations overall performance should be a permanent objective of the organisation.

B8 Principle 7 Factual approach to decision making

Effective decisions are based on analyses of data and information

B9 Principle 8 Mutually beneficial supplier relationships

An organisation and its suppliers are interdependent and a mutually beneficial relationship enhances the ability of both to create value.

As can be seen from above the eight management principles from "Vision 2000" form the fundamental structure and lifeblood to the ISO 9000 (FoS). The structure and format of ISO 9001 and ISO 9004 have been developed with the eight management principles in mind. It is interesting to see that there are just 8 principles. Yet they have and still do allow Quality Management to achieve its aim provided the use of the Standards is effective. As anyone who has read any of my books, articles and discussions will know I do not believe they are being used effectively. (See www.pdqms.co.uk for articles)

This document is an attempt to make people aware of what the ISO 9000 Family of Standards is and the documents that have been developed from these four standards.

To me, and many others, the number 8 has a very significant meaning. To some it brings luck, to others good fortune, however like most things the 8 principles have to be used effectively before any benefit can be accrued.

Strategy and Policy (5.0)

This covers the need to establish the organisations Strategy and Policies in order to get the mission, vision and values accepted and supported by its interested parties.

It states that in this Standard a mission is a description of why an organisation exists, and a vision describes its state, i.e. what the organisation wants to be and how it wants to be seen by its interested parties.

Definitions

Vision
- The ability to see what will happen in the future (To see where you would wish to be) **Note:**—A Vision is not measurable at the time

Mission
- A number of persons entrusted with work. A company's mission is simply the **main objective/s** to be teased out of the vision with identification of who will do it.

Objective
- Relating to or constituting an object
- Existing or considered only in relation to your mind
- **Something you wish to achieve/reach**

Policy
- The art of government/Statecraft
- **A course of action**
- **System of administration guided more by "Interest" than by "Principle"**

Strategy
- General-ship or the art of conducting a campaign and manoeuvring an army

Strategic
- Pertaining to dictated by

Strategic position
- One that gives you strength

Tactics
- Adroit management of situation (Adroit = Dexterous, skilful, ingenious)

Procedure
- Method of conducting business
- Course of action
- A step taken or an act performed

Considered Options

        Vision—Where you see yourself being

        Mission—The main objective/s that you need to obtain to attain your vision

        Objective—What you are there to achieve

        Policy—The course of action guided more by interest than by principle

        Strategy—How you are going to carry out your campaign taking into account Policy and Objectives

Resource Management (6.0)

This requires the organisation to identify the internal and external resources that are needed for the achievement of the organisations objectives in the short and long term.

The resources cover everything from people, equipment, facilities, materials, energy, knowledge, finance as well as infrastructure, suppliers and partners.

In fact it covers everything that could affect the organisation's ability to be successful. It includes looking at Risks and Opportunities. It even covers natural resources including the integration of environmental protection aspects into product design and development as well as to the developing processes to mitigate risks.

As can be seen this takes the whole activity outside the limited concerns of ISO 9001.

Process Management (7.0)

Processes are specific to an organisation and vary depending on the type size and level of maturity of the organisation. It drives management to be proactive in looking at their processes including outsourced processes to ensure they are effective and efficient. There is even a note in the general section that can guide you to further information on the "Process Approach" from other documents within Annex B already mentioned as well as other ISO 9000 "Introduction and Support package document.

Monitoring, Measurement, analysis and review. (8.0)

To achieve sustained success in an ever changing and uncertain environment, it is necessary for the organisation to regularly monitor, measure, analyses and review its performance. Whereas ISO 9001 restricts itself to the product realisation process ISO 9004 broadens this to all aspects of its management activity.

It covers the broader Key Performance Indicators (KPI), self assessment, benchmarking to mention a few techniques.

Improvement, innovation and learning (9.0)

Depending on the organisations environment, improvement and innovation could be necessary for sustained success.

The whole of the document gives many ideas and guidance on how to achieve success. It could be useful to any organisation whatever its size and business.

If what you have read is of interest then I suggest you obtain ISO 9004 and identify which part of the Standard would benefit your organisation.

ISO 9004 is a very detailed and useful standard if you wish to manage all the business activities in an effective manner. Why would any Organisation ignore this opportunity to apply the tried and tested techniques in ISO 9004?

7.0 ISO 19011 2011 Guidelines for auditing management systems

The index for both ISO 19011 2002 and 2011 is similar with just section 6 of the main headings changed from Audit Activities (2002) to Performing an Audit (2011). The changes came in the sub clauses. See below section 5 to7.

1.0 Scope is very similar in that it covers the same ground however the new standard has been broadened from auditing the Quality and Environmental management standards of 2002 to the auditing of any management system 2011. It still highlights that it can cover other types of audit in principle provided that special consideration is paid to the competence of the audit team members.

2.0 Normative references. This section indicates that there are no applicable standards that should be referred to and misses out on any reference to ISO 9000 Fundamentals and vocabulary that was in the previous issue. This seems a simplistic approach bought on by the failure of Quality professionals to refer to the definitions in ISO 9000. The previous ISO 19011 2002 did identify ISO 9000 as a normative reference as did the other ISO 9000 (FoS). A recent survey indicated that 70% of ISO 9001 Certified Organisations do not even have ISO 9000 despite the fact that ISO 9001 section 2 Normative references stating that ISO 9000 is **indispensable** to the application of ISO 9001. This once again highlights that the ISO 9001 clauses 1-3 are generally ignored when carrying out ISO 9001 Certification Audits. If ISO 9001 clause 4.2.3f is to being applied correctly then ISO 9000 would be a standard held by the organisation or how else can the organisation comply with ISO 9001.

KEY 23 In the latest issue of ISO 19011 Section 2 it excludes ISO 9000 as a normative reference. This undermines the whole logic of ISO 19011 being in the ISO 9000 Family of Standards (FoS).

3.0 It is interesting to note that some of the definitions in ISO 9000 are repeated word for word in section 3 Terms and Definitions of ISO 19011. It is also of note that there is no stated commitment in ISO 19011 Section 2 Normative References (above) to using ISO 9000 and this is a change from the previous version (2002). Does this mean all other Standards relating to the ISO 9000 (FoS) will also have no Normative reference to ISO 9000? This omission seems to indicate that the terminology being used in Quality is selective rather than definitive and that approach supports the people who argue that it doesn't matter what something is called. No wonder we have confusion when they use any term they like with no consideration to the International nature of the standard and the role of ISO 9000.

4.0 Principles of Auditing. There has been one new requirement added to the 5 previous principles related to auditors and that is Confidentiality. There was also one change in title and that is from Ethical Conduct to Integrity. The six are now, Fair Presentation, Due Professional Care, Confidentiality, Independence and Evidence Base Approach all of which are explained in ISO 19011.

5.0 Managing an audit programme. This is very similar and again highlights the use of the PDCA from the previous 2002 version as mentioned before. This is broken down into the individual explanations for each sector of the process. 5.1 General Activities is described by text. The next are in the format of a flow chart 5.2 and 5.3 are part of the (PLAN). 5.4 is conducting the audit (DO) 5.5 is monitoring the audit programme (CHECK) and 5.6 Reviewing and improving the audit programme is (ACT). This is all to do with the audit programme itself not the method of carrying out an audit.

6.0 Audit activities. This is where the actual auditing activities comes in and is in a flow chart format except for 6.1 General which explains that the flow chart provides an overview of the typical auditing activity adding that the sequence can differ. The flow chart starts with 6.2 Initiating the Audit, The old document review had its own separate box but this is now included in 6.3 Preparing Audit Activities as that includes document review, audit plan etc. 6.4 Conducting the Audit, 6.5 Preparing and Distributing the Audit Report 6.6 Completing the Audit then finishing with Conducting an Audit Follow Up if required. This flow chart is followed by a detailed explanation about each activity identified within the process. The detail in this has been modified with the clauses renumbered but generally covers the same activity.

7.0 Competence and evaluation of auditors. The one area this standard really misses out on is the competence of the people and the method of judging competence. The standard of auditor competence in some countries across the world is quite low and what is accepted as an audit does not achieve the purpose or scope of ISO 9001. In many cases it is just checking to see if the clauses 4-8 of the ISO 9001 standard are covered within the Management System not whether that process actually does achieve what it should achieve.

In many cases the decision is made that it is not working well we need to write another Standard. Once again we get the proliferation of Standards.

This brings to mind the current need to rewrite Standards because they are not clear. I had this given to me recently and it does make a complete nonsense over the EU need for detailed regulations. Is quality going the same way?

Pythagoras' theorem:	24 words.
Lord's Prayer:	66 words.
Archimedes' Principle:	67 words.
10 Commandments:	179 words.
Gettysburg address:	286 words.
US Declaration of Independence:	1,300 words.
US Constitution with all 27 Amendments:	7,818 words.

HOWEVER:—

EU regulations on the sale of cabbage   26,911 words

NOTE:—Words not counted by me so please no corrections.

ISO 9000 (FoS) has been revised a few times. Does it make it clearer?

Some people indicate that ISO 9001 is not clear. Of course it is clear if you refer back to the purpose and scope of the standard and then apply it appropriately to the Organisation's business. ISO 9001 is still capable of achieving the purpose if it is used effectively.

COMPETENCE

ISO 19011 now has a separate sub clause to determine auditor competence. However, the ability to judge competence is still an issue that has not been resolved. Some auditors do not understand the purpose of carrying out an audit. This needs to be addressed if audits are to regain credibility. Auditors are not there to audit the organisations procedures to see if they are being followed, they are there to see if the processes being followed are capable of consistently achieving the required output. Auditors that do not carry out process audits cannot be considered competent. Yes procedures and other documented systems are important but the auditor should be auditing the process using whatever management system is in place to judge if the processes are effective.

APPENDICES

ISO 19011 Appendices are guidance documents and do give information on conducting document review, sampling, preparing work documents, selecting sources of information etc and are useful. What is disappointing is the failure to major on process audits following an audit trail. (See Appendix B of this document)

In the drive to bring RISK into auditing it has failed to understand that RISK should be clearly identified within the Standard that the audit is being carried out against. Only two standards in the ISO 9000 (FoS) should contain "Risk" they are ISO 9004 and ISO 19011. If it is introduced across the board it could imply a change in the scope of ISO 9001 by bringing "RISK" in as a specific clause. This would confuse the purpose of the ISO 9001 Management System as it would lead to mixed messages that could take the Standard from a simple Management System for meeting customer requirements into a much broader management activity.

Once again this highlights the failure to understand the purpose of ISO 9001. No one can deny that meeting the customer's requirements is important to customer satisfaction. We should all remember the term:—

"THE CUSTOMER IS KING"

The reason ISO 9001 (BS 5750) Certification was introduced was to mitigate risk by applying an effective Management System that could be assessed both by the Organisation and any party auditing that Management System to see if the Quality Management System was able to demonstrate its ability to consistently provide product that meets customer and applicable statutory and regulatory requirements. It is this failure in auditor training that has allowed auditors to believe they do not need to know what the product or service is when carrying out an audit. They have been taught that they are only checking to see if the management system has addressed clauses 4-8 of ISO 9001 and this is called a system audit.

SYSTEM AUDIT

How do I know this?

On the LinkedIn forum 50% of respondents did not believe that they needed to know what the outcome was supposed to be from the process they were auditing. The same percentage also indicated that only clauses 4-8 were relevant to an ISO 9001 audit. How, with this level of training, can anyone carrying out an audit believe that they are capable of judging if a Management System can consistently meet the customer's specified requirements? The term "A System Audit" was introduced to cover the above auditing approach. It ignores the fact that the system should actually achieve something or what is the point of it? Just having a documented system that "Ticks" all the boxes against the ISO clauses 4-8 of ISO 9001 does not and cannot ensure that the management system is effective.

When attending a UK Standards Development Group (SDG) meeting, there was a comment that the format for ISO standards was possibly going to be changed. Amongst other issues, a clause called "Risk" could be added. (Possibly "Risk and Opportunity") When challenged as being inappropriate for all standards it was stated that if "Risk" was not applicable the relevant standard could state that it is not applicable. It was pointed out that if a specific clause on Risk had been identified in the new format for ISO 9001 no one would support stating it was not applicable. The response made was in that case it must be relevant. In the Introduction to ISO 9001: 2008 clause 0.4 it states that the standard does not include requirements specific to other management systems one of which was Risk Management. **(See KEY 14)**. However this is conveniently ignored and glossed over. This drive to reformat and rewrite standards should be based on need. Trying to fit every standard into the same extended format only succeeds in increasing the content of the standard with, in many cases, no benefit. This will lead to compromise and confusing text. (See reference to EU regulations on the sale of Cabbages earlier page). Lets get "Back to Basics". (See www. pdqms.co.uk articles)

DEFINITIONS

There are also some definitions that have been put into ISO 19011 that are different to those in ISO 9000.

Let us look at some of these differences:—

Auditor

Auditor: The new definition in ISO 19011 misses out the first part of the ISO 9000:2005 definition namely: "person **with the demonstrated personal attributes and competence** (3.1.6 and 3.9.14) to conduct an audit".

Once again the ISO 9000:2005 gives the definition of competence as:—

Competence 3.1.6 demonstrated ability to apply knowledge and skills.

The fact that this has now been removed from ISO 19011 requirements is at least honest because I for one believe the current level of auditor competence is as low as it has ever been.

See ISO 9001 Audit Trail book that was developed from the article Audit Trail Appendix B (sample of Audit Trail is attached Appendix E).

The definition in ISO 19011 now uses just the first and last three words.

Auditor: "Person who conducts an audit" and then references "audit" clause (3.1) in ISO 19011.(No need for competence then?)

Considering one of the most critical complaints about auditors is the lack of competence this seems like a significant step backward. Why would you remove **with the demonstrated attributes and competence?** I would love to know others views on the revised definition for auditor as given in ISO 19011. It seems like the same logic behind considering doing away with "Preventive Action" in ISO 9001 because no one understands it.

Sorry, I, and many others do understand the difference between Preventive and Corrective Action and actually teach the difference. Why don't others teach the requirements of the Standard correctly? If the words in ISO 9000 for Corrective and Preventive Action are carefully read through then there should be no confusion.

Audit Criteria

Audit Criteria has also been changed however all it has done is include the Note below the definition ISO 9000:2005 into the new definition in ISO 19011.

It is not the intention to go through all the modifications that have occurred in ISO 19011 Section 3 Terms and Definitions. The purpose is to highlight some of these anomalies and point out that they are not a sensible approach within the ISO 9000 (FoS). Why not just identify ISO:9000 as a Normative reference then all the repetition in ISO 19011 would be unnecessary? I am sure other definitions in ISO 9000 are used but not defined. The reason for this change does not seem obvious. This is another reason for writing this document covering the ISO 9000 (FoS), because the approach being taken at present is undermining the family of standards as illustrated by the failure to reference ISO 9000 in the Normative references in ISO 19011. Will the same approach be taken when revising ISO 9001? I do hope not or what will happen to the ISO 9000 (FoS)?

KEY 24 Changes to ISO 9000 definitions should only be defined in another quality standard where there is no definition in ISO 9000 or the definition that does exist does not meet the meaning within that standard.

This approach would allow the definitions proposed in any other Quality Standard to be considered for inclusion in ISO 9000 when ISO 9000 is up for revision. I can only hope that this would allow competent Quality personnel to block pointless changes.

I had hoped that the Quality professionals who stated that they supported the term "Audit Trail" would have pushed the need to have a definition. If auditors (Old definition) could understand the importance of Process audits following an Audit Trail then I believe the standard of auditing would improve. While the "Tick Box" fraternity rule there is no chance of improving the credibility of auditing no matter how many standards are written or how many extra clauses are added.

The majority of audit requirements are not dissimilar to the previous version. The interesting thing is ISO 19011 Clause 7 covers competence and evaluation of auditors. This does question the logic behind changing the definition for Auditor.

KEY 25 Why has the definition for auditor in ISO 19011:2012 removed the requirement for "Demonstrated personal attributes and competence "from the current ISO 9000:2005 definition?

It is defined as:—

person who conducts an audit (ISO 19011:2011)
OR
person with the demonstrated personal attributes and competence to conduct an audit (ISO 9000:2005)

There has been a great many discussions on auditor competence however the standard controlling auditing has decided to drop the personal attributes and competence from the definition in ISO 19011?

If the approach taken with ISO 19011 is taken across other standards when they are revised the ability to have a common definitive definition across all the standards will be lost.

KEY 26 The central control of Quality related definitions through ISO 9000 is being undermined and individuals on each standard committee will be able to develop their own definitions with no reference to the core definitions within ISO 9000. Is this acceptable?

The questions in KEY 25 and KEY 26 are
INTERESTING QUESTION TO FINISH ON
Maybe the above questions fully justify the development
of this document?

8.0 CONCLUSIONS

8.1 ISO 9000 Family of Standards (FoS)

The three Standards, ISO 9000, 9001 and 9004, form a coherent Family of Standards that has been developed to assist organisations, of all types and sizes, to implement and operate effective Quality Management Systems.

8.2 Knowledge of ISO 9000 Family of Standards

The failure to train quality personnel on the purpose of the family of standards has led to confusion in their use. This affects ISO 9001 where there is a continual drive to add inappropriate clauses that belong in ISO 9004 ignoring the limited scope of ISO 9001.

8.3 ISO 19011:2011 (Normative References)

ISO 19011 is a guidance document that is currently defined as part of the ISO 9000 Family of Standards (FoS). The latest version (2011) no longer references ISO 9000 in its normative references leaving a concern that ISO 19011 is no longer part of the ISO 9000 Family of Standards.

8.4 ISO 19011:2011 Guidelines for auditing management systems

ISO 19011 majors on how to manage an Audit with limited information on how to perform an audit. The fact that many auditors do not carry out process audits affects auditor competence. The definition for "auditor" in ISO 19011 has been modified from the ISO 9000 definition because it has removed the term "Competence" from ISO 19001 section 3 Terms and definitions. This is counterproductive.

8.5 Use of the ISO 9000 Family of standards (FoS).

The minimum recommended (FoS) required by an organisation are **ISO 9000 and ISO 9001 as they are recognised as a matched pair.** The two complement each other and ensure that the purpose, usage and terminology are explained and clarified.

8.6 ISO 9004

Is usually implemented after the benefits of ISO 9001 have been achieved. Namely the organisations ability to consistently provide product or service that meets the customer and statutory and regulatory requirements. In effect ISO 9004 fills the gap left by the restrictive scope of ISO 9001 and enables the organisation to build for sustained success. This can only be achieved when the organisation looks at all issues that affect its business. ISO 9004 gives them the tools to do that.

8.7 Use of the ISO 9000 Family of Standards and their clauses in isolation

The biggest problem that undermines the credibility of the ISO 9000 Family is that the Standards are looked at in isolation. The same problem occurs when organisations look at each clause in isolation as if the only purpose is to comply with the clause. The actual benefit of using the ISO 9000 Family of Standards (FoS) is missed.

I can only hope that this document will enable organisations to see the benefit of applying the ISO 9000 Family of Standards to the benefit of their businesses. I accept that many people may disagree all I can hope is it gets discussion going before ISO 9000 and ISO 9001 are revised.

9.0 FINAL THOUGHTS

9.1 The ISO 9001 standard is now used by many organisations and because of this there is a drive to add more to the standard as it has a large audience.

This should cause considerable concern especially as the Certification scheme is not always achieving the purpose of the standard.

9.2 ISO 9001 Certification is to give confidence to the Organisation and the buyers who use that Organisation's service that Certified Organisations are able to consistently provide product that meets the customer and statutory and regulatory requirements. The current approach does not achieve that, especially when Auditors indicate there is no need to know what the product or service is.

9.3 To enable **Certification Bodies** to survive in a competitive environment they are having to reduce their prices. One way of doing this is to reduce the number of man-days. In many cases the time allotted for the auditor to carry out an audit and judge if the Management systems and processes are capable of consistently providing products that meet the customer's requirements is compromised.

9.4 Certified Organisations have a role to play as they need to understand the benefits of using the ISO 9000 Family of standards. If the standard of auditing could be improved (Not "Tick Box" against clauses) Professional process audits following an audit trail will gather information that can help organisations improve.

9.5 Attached to this document Appendix C is a proposed **improvement project**. It will take 5 years and is a SMART improvement in that it is Specific, Measurable, Achievable, Realistic and Timely. Please see if you believe that the credibility of auditing could be improved if this improvement proposal was implemented?

9.6 The ISO 9000 Family of standards can help any organisation improve with or without certification. I suspect that if ISO 9001 is revised and "Risk", which is not relevant to ISO 9001, is added many Organisations will show their displeasure and move away from certification

9.7 There should be nothing wrong with **Certification Bodies** carrying out audits of certified organisations against relevant requirements from ISO 9004 provided they are open and honest about it. **Audits to ISO 9004 cannot be certified**, however they could help organisations manage for the sustained success of their business. The current approach of trying to add ISO 9004 requirements under the banner of ISO 9001 certification is not helpful as many audits that are carried out at present cannot even achieve the basic purpose and scope of ISO9001 namely consistently meeting customer requirements.

9.8 My hope is that there will be a drive to **improve the standard of auditing**. Previously I only discussed ISO 9001 and I found it difficult to get my concerns across, as many individuals were not willing to reconsider what is currently taking place and its effectiveness. I am hoping that in going **"Back to Basics"** looking at the purpose and scope of all the ISO 9000 Family of Standards the original intention will become clearer. This may lead to a better use of ISO 9000 family of standards to the benefit of all.

APPENDIX A

OTHER QUALITY DOCUMENTS THAT MAY BE RELATED OR PROVIDE GUIDANCE TO THE ISO 9000 FAMILY OF STANDARDS

Many of these documents have been developed on the back of the ISO 9000 Family of Standards (FoS) and as such should NOT be considered part of the (FoS) but the next level down in hierarchy. Some standards have become a specific requirement for a particular industry. Where this occurs they are normally structured against the requirements within ISO 9001 and cover specific industry needs.

Note: abbreviated titles used to simplify the list but give information on usage.

ISO 10001	Customer satisfaction—codes of conduct for organisations
ISO 10002	Customer satisfaction—complaints handling in organisations.
ISO 10003	Customer satisfaction—dispute resolution external organisations.
ISO 10004	Customer satisfaction—guidelines for monitoring and measuring
ISO 10005	Guidelines for quality plans
ISO 10006	Quality management in projects
ISO 10007	For configuration management
ISO 10012	Measurement processes and measuring equipment **(Requirement)**
ISO 10013	Quality management system documentation
ISO 10014	Realising financial and economic benefits
ISO 10015	Quality management training
ISO 10017	Statistical techniques for ISO 9001

ISO 10019	Selection of QMS consultants and use of their services
ISO/TC 16949	Requirements for ISO 9001 for automotive production and service parts (**Requirement rather than guide**)
AS 9100	Aerospace QMS requirements for design, development. Production installation and servicing (Based on ISO 9001 **Requirement**)
ISO 22000	Food safety management systems
ISO 15378	Primary packaging materials for medicinal products covering good manufacturing practices (GMP)
ISO 22006	The application of ISO 9001:2008 to crop production
ISO/IEC	90003 Software engineering guidelines to computer software
ISO/IECNP90006	Application of ISO 9001 to IT service management
ISOTR 90005	Application of ISO 9001 to systems life cycle processes
IWA 2: 2007	Application for ISO 9001:2000 in education
IWA 4:2009	Application of ISO 9001:2008 in local government
TickIT	Guide to software QMS construction and certification.

There are many other national or international management systems not necessarily linked to quality that may need to be considered dependent on the type of business your Organisation is in.

BS EN 12798	Transport Road Rail and Inland waterways
BS EN 60300	Dependability management
ISO 13485	Medical devices
ISO 14001	Environmental management systems

ISO 22000	Food safety management for organisation sin the food chain
ISO 28000	Specification for security management systems
ISO/CDTS 29001	Petroleum, Petrochemical and natural gas industries.
ISO/IEC 27001	Information technology—security techniques—etc
OHSAS 18001	Occupational health and safety management systems

Note 1:—The above is not a full definitive list but a guide on what else could be applicable dependent on the organisations business.

These documents are subject to change so please check latest issue

Note 2:—See next page for proposed documented structure for ISO Quality Standards.

Appendix A Proposal

Possible Structure for the ISO 9000 Family of Standards (FoS) And ISO Quality Requirements and Guidance Standards

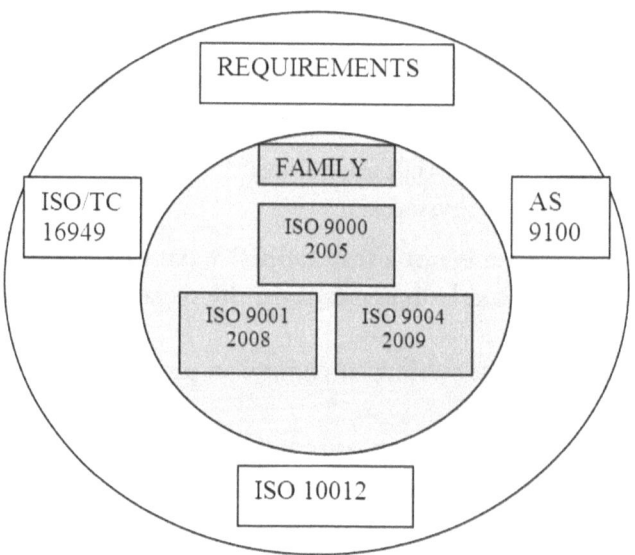

STRUCTURE

Inner ring covers the ISO 9000 Family of standards

2nd Ring   Covers Quality Standards that are Requirements

3rd Ring (Not Shown) Covers Guidance Documents

4th Ring (If needed) Covers more detailed supporting documents

The above is just a proposed structure that hopefully will prevent the current drive to include all quality related documents within the ISO 9000 Family of Standards.

I am sure there are people on committees who are better placed than I am to decide on which standard should go where.

As you may have noticed ISO 19011 has been removed and if the documented structure above was implemented it would be in the 3rd Ring as a guidance document.

APPENDIX B

International Organization for Standardization

International Accreditation Forum

Date: 10 December 2009

ISO 9001 AUDITING PRACTICES GROUP GUIDANCE ON: AUDIT TRAIL

The following paper by David John Seear is adapted from an article in IRCA's **INform** journal (Issue No.24, December 2009, http://www.irca.org/inform/issue24/Seear.html)

1. Introduction

There are numerous important elements to carrying out a professional audit. Some requirements, such as the need to audit the process, are defined in ISO 9000. There is, however, one element of auditing that is missing in the terms and definitions in ISO 9000—the *audit trail*.

The failure to carry out a process audit following an audit trail is the single most important reason why audits are not effective.

2. What is an audit trail?

In the absence of a definition from ISO 9000, a standard dictionary definition for 'audit' and 'trail' arrives at the following:

A systematic approach to collecting evidence based on specific samples, that the output of a series of inter-related processes meets expected outcomes.

But what does this mean in practice?

Although applied by some auditors, the use of an audit trail is by no means universally accepted. It is the failure to ensure all audits employ process audits following an audit trail that undermines their credibility. Auditors should understand the path of the process that they are auditing and perform the audit accordingly, ensuring that the requirements of the process are being met.

For example, as a matter of course auditors will visit the shop floor. This enables the auditor to see what is taking place and to identify the specific order numbers of jobs that are going through at that time. From this information it is easy to identify in the sales department the agreed specification for that product or service and select relevant samples to be chosen. This means the process can be checked to ensure that what takes place is controlled and will meet the required specification. From here, the audit trail is picked up and followed through.

Using the audit of a purchasing activity as an example, you need to identify what material or equipment has been purchased for your sample order. It is always important to understand what drives the process. In this case, it is normally the requisition, which defines what is wanted.

If the auditor does not understand the specification, then he or she cannot check if the process being followed meets the requirements of the requisition.

- what does the requisition require—does this comply with the agreed specification?

- how is the decision to purchase made?
- how is the specification decided? Is it adequate?
- who decides what is required and do they have the authority?
- who chooses the supplier and by what criteria?
- what is the process for bid evaluation?
- how is the specification advised to the supplier?
- are national or international standards used?
- what controls the process?
- are there any special packing delivery requirements?

These are just some of the issues that need to be addressed, many of which follow the clauses of ISO 9001.

3. Correct samples

The starting point for the audit is to use the chosen samples and identify the process path and the controls that were applied. It is vital that the samples are linked and come from the same trail. Too frequently, audit samples are taken at different stages of the process and are not related or linked to the initial sample chosen, which means that an auditor is unable to verify that the process is working. He will only be able to check if that particular document is filled in correctly.

Procedures, forms, checklists and so on, all ensure that a process is managed and controlled effectively. It is essential that auditors take the time to understand what is required from the process they are auditing.

It is impossible for a second—or third-party auditor to carry out an audit of an organization if the auditor does not take the time to understand the specification of its product or service, including statutory and regulatory requirements. It is this professional approach to auditing that allows the auditor to identify any weaknesses in the process and decide if an organization is capable of meeting the specified requirements. The audit trail approach applies to any audit be it an internal, second—or third-party audit.

About the author

David John Seear C. Eng. (daveseear@btinternet.com) spent 12 years at sea, where he reached the position of Chief Engineer, followed by 20 years with Shell UK, where he was appointed as 'Head of Quality and Performance' for Shell UK Materials. He represented the UK on ISO /TC176 for 3 years, as well as representing the Confederation of British Industry on the UK's mirror committee to ISO/TC 176. He now runs PDQ Management Services.

For further information on the ISO 9001 Auditing Practices Group, please refer to the paper:

Introduction to the ISO 9001 Auditing Practices Group

Feedback from users will be used by the *ISO 9001 Auditing Practices Group* to determine whether additional guidance documents should be developed, or if these current ones should be revised.

The other ISO 9001 Auditing Practices Group papers and presentations may be downloaded from the web sites:

www.iaf.nu
www.iso.org/tc176/ISO9001AuditingPracticesGroup

Disclaimer

This paper has not been subject to an endorsement process by the International Organization for Standardization (ISO), ISO Technical Committee 176, or the International Accreditation Forum (IAF).

The information contained within it is available for educational and communication purposes. The *ISO 9001 Auditing Practices Group* does not take responsibility for any errors, omissions or other liabilities that may arise from the provision or subsequent use of such information.

APPENDIX C

PROPOSED FIVE YEAR
IMPROVEMENT PROJECT

Revision 2012

Programme so far:—

1. www.irca.org/inform/issue24/Seear.html   published   10th December 2009. This article on Audit Trail was written with the intention of improving audits.
2. This was also picked up by www.iso/tc176/ ISO9001AuditingPracticesGroup who published the same article but with a modified definition for Audit Trail. It was nice to see that the APB acknowledged the article came from IRCA.
3. Feed back from the articles led to the issue of ISO 9001 Audit Trail in March 2010 (Paperback and Pamphlet).www.pdqms. co.uk
4. Four articles have been published in Quality World. The first entitled Audit Trail, which led to the articles in 1 and 2 above. The second on Auditing the standard (QW June 2010), "Tick Box" mentality (QW November 2010) Letter of the month January 2011 And then "Back to Basics February 2011.
5. All the above are on the same theme. Letters have been written to UKAS, CQI and IRCA about an improvement however there has only been a response from UKAS who responded saying they wished me well with the task and suggested they would help where they could.
6. This now leads to the annual review of the progress so far. Discussions in IRCA's LinkedIn lead me to believe there is still up to 50% of the auditing personnel who believe, as I do, that auditing should be improved. This has led me to believe that, although difficult, it should not be impossible.

Improvement Plan 2012:—

1. The first activity in the plan is to improve the quality of the Auditor Training. The four key elements that need to be re-emphasised are:—
   a. Remind everyone ISO 9001 is a Tool not an Objective
   b. The statutory and regulatory requirements in ISO 9001 are only those applicable to the product
   c. All audits should be process audits following an audit trail.
   d. The purpose of an audit is to see if the processes can consistently meet specified requirements.
2. It is important that IRCA assessors of Internal and Lead Auditor training courses are reminded of what they should look for in the IRCA approved Audit Courses. (See 1 above) that would ensure these messages get across. Many training courses do include Audit Trail but IRCA should push TC 176/sc1 and ensure they include a definition of Audit Trail in ISO 9000 when it is revised. A good start would be to use either of the definitions from the APB version or the IRCA Inform Issue 24 version.
3. A new 1 day Auditor training course covering the ISO 9000 Family of Standards should be developed covering the four standards. It would also allow improvement in the quality of the auditing that takes place as auditing techniques could be included. This would bring credibility back to ISO 9001 auditing activities.
4. At some time during 2013 accreditation bodies and others should be reminding everyone what ISO 9001 certification should achieve. Indicating that a 3 year project starting in 2013 would be introduced. I will not go into detail at this point. This would lay the foundation for the improvement project.

Improvement Plan 2012-2017:—

1. The important point here is to indicate that during the first three year period no ISO 9001 Certified Organisation will loose there ISO 9001 certificate because of this change and

there will be a further year (2017) where certification bodies can use their discretion.

2. What will happen is Certification Bodies will be advised that where an Organisation has weaknesses that can impact on their ability to meet the customer, statutory and regulatory specifications for the product they will be rated. This rating will be A, B and C. This will, during the initial three year period, be confidential to the Certified Organisation. (Details of how this works is available but will not be discussed here).

3. Even this approach, having seen it work in practice, will encourage Certified Organisations to improve the ability of their systems, processes and facilities etc. (No one likes to be lower than an "A"). Again a Win-Win situation.

4. The way in which the Certification Auditing will work is that during the three year auditing period one of the audits possibly the tri-annual visit will be specifically targeted at the Product or Service only. It is this audit that must have competent person who knows the Product/Service area and can add value. This should cause no problem to Competent Professional Certification Bodies. It does mean that the other audits may during this initial period be carried out in a similar manner as that used now.

5. I do recognise that some Certification Bodies do these types of audits anyway and again they should not loose out.

6. As already indicated 2017 will be the year where the final tidying up will take place. By that time all auditors should understand that ISO 9001 audits are to see if the Organisations Systems demonstrate its ability to consistently provide product that meets customer and applicable statutory and regulatory requirements. It is not about auditing to see if the ISO 9001 clauses 4-8 are included in the Organisations management system as this achieves very little.

As IRCA published the first article on "Audit Trail" I trust that this proposal would be of interest to all quality professionals and could be pursued with the hope of bringing credibility back to ISO 9001 auditing. If ISO 9001 audits are carried out in a more professional manner then Certified Organisation will gain by having their strengths and weaknesses highlighted enabling them to see where they are and improve where necessary.

Failing this I would ask a National Accreditation Body or the International Accreditation Body (IAF) to recognise the problem and take action.

I can only trust that this proposal will be met with a sympathetic hearing.

It should be recognised that ISO 9001 is just one tool in a Quality professional's toolbox and the whole ISO 9000 Family of standards should be taught to all Quality professional. In this way it should retain its role in ensuring that products meet specified requirements.

As you can see I have not given up hope yet.

Kind Regards

David John Seear

APPENDIX D

KEY POINTS

KEY 1 The ISO 9000 Family of Standards (FoS) consists of ISO 9000, ISO 9001, ISO 9004 and ISO 19011.

KEY 2 The eight management principles should be referred to when interpreting what is required within the ISO 9000 Family of Standards (FoS).

KEY 3 Training in the purpose and use of the ISO 9000 Family of Standards (FoS) should be carried out if the benefit of the Family is to be obtained.

KEY 4 Organisations should understand the value of documentation where it is needed to enable communication of intent and consistency of action

KEY 5 The quality management system (QMS) is the organizations management system and does not have a separate life of its own.

KEY 6 Management review is the opportunity to gather information and make decisions on how to improve the Organisations processes and activities.

KEY 7 Introducing other terms to ISO 9000, such as Stakeholder, when there already is a term for "Interested Parties" should not be contemplated. The term Stakeholder should go into the standard to which it is relevant, which is ISO 9004.

KEY 8 ISO 9000 should be in every Quality Professional's tool kit or how else will Quality Professionals talk the same language?

KEY 9 ISO 9001, 9004 and ISO 19011 should all state, in section 2.0 of each standard, that ISO 9000 is a Normative Reference or how could they be considered part of the same Family of Standards (FoS).

KEY 10 The Statutory and regulatory requirements, as far as ISO 9001 is concerned, are only those statutory and regulatory requirements that relate directly to the product.

KEY 11 The ISO 9000 Family of standards should NOT be extended beyond the current four standards of ISO 9000, ISO 900, ISO 9004 and ISO 19011.

KEY 12 Audits should be process audits following an audit trail or it is not possible to verify if a process is effective in meeting the required output.

KEY 13 The ISO 9001 standard restricts its scope to the management system that directly relates to meeting the customer and applicable statutory and regulatory requirements.

KEY 14 The ISO 9001 standard does NOT include other management systems such as, Environmental, Occupational Health and Safety, Finance and Risk Management.

KEY 15 Remember ISO 9001 clause 1.1 Note 1, The term product only applies to product intended for, or required by a customer or any intended output resulting from the product realisation processes.

KEY 16 The key processes for product/service delivery is section 7 Product Realisation with, as required, able support from the other clauses.

KEY 17 The Organisation is responsible for developing a management system that meets their requirements not the Certification Body.

KEY 18 Outsourcing any activity that could affect the organisations ability to meet the customers requirements does not absolve the Organisation from that responsibility

KEY 19. The quality manual is a commitment that explains WHAT the organisation does. It does not have to include the Why, When, How, Where and Who.

KEY 20 The ISO 9001 quality management has only one restrictive purpose and that is to manage the processes controlling the business directly linked to providing the product/service that meets the customer's requirements.

KEY 21 When using each clause it should be referred back to the ISO 9001 scope if it is to be interpreted correctly.

KEY 22 Information = Meaningful Data (ISO 9000:2005) management review without meaningful data (information) is of no use.

KEY 23 In the latest issue of ISO 19011 Section 2 it excludes ISO 9000 as a normative reference. This undermines the whole logic of ISO 19011 being in the ISO 9000 Family of Standards (FoS).

KEY 24 Changes to ISO 9000 definitions should only be defined in another quality standard where there is no definition in ISO 9000 or the definition that does exist does not meet the meaning within that standard.

KEY 25 Why has the definition for auditor in ISO 19011:2011 removed the requirement for "Demonstrated personal attributes and competence" from the current ISO 9000:2005 definition?

KEY 26 The central control of Quality related definitions through ISO 9000 is being undermined and individuals on each standard committee will be able to develop their own definitions with no reference to the core definitions within ISO 9000. Is this acceptable?

>> ISO 9001 Audit Trail
A Practical Guide to Process Auditing
Following an Audit Trail

Price £10

APPENDIX E

FIRST EDITION ISO 9001 AUDIT TRAIL
MARCH 2010 (EXTRACTS)

INDEX

Note 1:—These are for information on how this document developed. Opinions are those of the author and may not necessarily be accepted by everyone.

Note 2:—Only the uneven sections in bold on the index are in this extract of the 1ˢᵗ Edition of the ISO 9001 Audit Trail book issued March 2010. The book is being revised and will be published last Quarter 2012. A limited number of 1ˢᵗ editions are available from www.pdqms.co.uk

Sections included are 1, 3, 5, 7, 9, 11, 13, Odd numbered Guidance Documents and Appendix A KEY Listing.

Audit Trail 1.0 Introduction

The article, explaining the importance of Process Audits following an "Audit Trail", was developed by David John Seear and has been accepted by the ISO 9001 Auditing Practice Group. It has also been highlighted in his letter in Quality World November 2009 and in a 700 word article published in the December 2009 issue of IRCA Inform, all of which address the topic and emphasises the importance of the "Audit Trail". This document has been developed following a request to expand this into a practical guide to auditing.

ISO 9001 is a tool—not an Objective. It is a tool for the Organisation to ensure that they have the systems in place to enable them to consistently provide a product/service that meets the specified requirements. It is also the criteria used by the Auditors to measure whether the Organisations have the Management System Requirements, Management Responsibilities, Resource Management, Product Realisation and finally the Measurement Analysis and Improvement in place to allow them to meet specified requirements and move forward.

KEY 1: REMEMBER ISO 9001 IS THE TOOL NOT THE OBJECTIVE

It is **NOT** the intention of this document to teach all the elements necessary to do a full professional audit, however the objective is to highlight the importance of a **"Process Audit following an Audit Trail"**. To achieve this the document has targeted sections of ISO 9001 Product Realisation (Primary Process) referencing some sections of 4, 5, 6 and 8 (Secondary processes) and the relevant parts of sections 1, 2 and 3 that are often glossed over.

1.1 Historic Terminology

The first thing to, remember without going back into history too far, is that the forerunner to ISO 9001 namely BS 5750 existed before Quality System Certification was introduced. In fact certification was introduced using BS 5750 and came in three parts. BS 5750 Part 1 that covered Organisations that carried out design. Part 2 covered Organisations that did not do design and Part 3 was for Organisations that only did Final Inspection. This approach allowed Purchasers to understand, from the type of certification given, what the Organisation was capable of doing.

The second thing to be aware of was ISO 9001: 2000 changed from a Purchasers standard to an Organisations standard.

The reason for this was prior to ISO 9001: 2000 the OLD terminology was:—

Purchaser—Supplier (Certified Organisation)—Sub Contractor

When ISO 9001:2000 was introduced the NEW terminology became:—

Customer—Organisation (Certified Organisation)—Supplier

Note:—The term Organisation in the ISO 9001 2000 version above is missing in ISO 9001 2008. Should this be reinstated when the ISO 9001 standard is revised in 2014?

The reason this was introduced in the year 2000 was there was considerable confusion over the original "Supplier"—"Sub Contractor" Terminology and because it was poorly taught it was not unusual to find Supplier (Old Terminology) even stated they did not use sub contractors when it meant suppliers who provided items to them. From a Purchaser's point of view the term Supplier (Certified Organisation) was correct because they were suppliers as far as the Purchaser was concerned.

The ISO 9001 standard is used in over 130 countries and as such it was more easily understood with the revised terminology as all Certified Organisations understood suppliers as being any one who supplied them.

This terminology linked with the removal of ISO 9001 Part 2 and Part 3 reduced the benefit for the Purchasers and is why it is not now a Purchaser's standard as information has been reduced.

It is the intention of this document to highlight that Independent ISO 9001 Certification should still give Purchasers confidence that their specified requirements can be met.

1.2 Reason certification was Introduced

The second thing to understand is why BS 5750 (ISO 9001) Certification was introduced. It was primarily introduced to stop or reduce multiple assessments. It was felt that an independent Accreditation Body approving Certification Bodies who in turn carried out Audits on Suppliers (Old Terminology) Organisations (Current terminology) would achieve this.

I will not go into the detail of why this was raised, however it was supported by the British Government as it was deemed <u>unnecessary</u> for British Industry to have numerous supplier audits taking place as it took up time, resources and in most cases was simple repetition as far as the Organisation (Current Terminology) was concerned.

Unfortunately, although this reduction in audits did occur, Purchaser confidence in Certification Audits has diminished and is now at an all time low. (2009)

On the CQI website (2009) is the Chartered Quality Institute (CQI) position regarding third party certification to ISO 9001

For purchasing organisations:

- **Third party certification to ISO 9001 is not a guarantee that a supplier will provide the quality of service or product specified by customers.**

PDQ Comment It can be accepted that this is not something that can be guaranteed, however the certification body carrying out the audit should be auditing to see if the Organisation is capable of consistently providing products or services that meet the specified requirements. This is stated at the top of the next CQI paragraph below.

- **Third party certification to ISO 9001 should provide confidence that the supplier has a management system that is focused on consistently providing their customers with conforming products and services. However, there is still significant variation in the quality and value of third party certifications carried out by the various certification bodies across the world and for this reason some purchasing organisations have reduced confidence in ISO 9001 certification.**

PDQ Comment

It is this lack of understanding of what ISO 9001 Certification is about that is the reason for developing this document highlighting the importance of the **AUDIT TRAIL** with the intention of improving the credibility of Internal Audits (1st Party), Vendor/Supplier Audits (2nd party) and Audits carried out by Certification Bodies (3rd Party).

The reason this situation has developed is mainly due to lack of understanding regarding what should be done during an Audit. There are some Auditors who believe that they are there to audit to see if the supplier's management system complies with ISO 9001.

As you can see from above this is totally untrue.

KEY 2:—It should be recognised that some purchasing Organisations have reduced confidence in ISO 9001 Certification

KEY 3:—All Audits should give the audited Organisation information about how robust their systems are in ensuring that they can consistently meet the required specification.

1.3 Objective and Purpose of ISO 9001

This brings us to the final important requirement and that is:—

The ISO 9001 Standard is a Tool Not an Objective.

ISO 9001 Sect 1.1 General states:—

a) This International Standard specifies requirements for a quality management system where an Organisation:—n**eeds to demonstrate its ability to consistently provide product that meets customer and applicable statutory and regulatory requirements**

b) and aims to enhance customer satisfaction through the effective application of the system, including processes for continual improvement of the system and the assurance of conformity to customer and applicable statutory and regulatory requirements.

There are also important notes

Note 1 In this International Standard the term "Product" only applies to

a) product intended for, or required by a customer
b) any intended output resulting from the product realisation processes.

Note 2 Statutory and regulatory requirements can be expressed as legal requirements

KEY 4:—From the above it is obvious that all auditing is about ensuring that the organisation can consistently meet the specified requirements.

The ISO 9001 standard is designed to provide a cross reference to relevant clauses so that when applied sensibly to any Organisation's Management System it will ensure that the product meets the specified requirements.

KEY 5:—There is still a belief that that Audits are to see if the ISO 9001 Certification clauses are covered within the Organisations Management System. This is incorrect as it conveys little or no information on how effective the processes are.

Introductory Conclusion

The above explains why this document was introduced following the Audit Trail articles published in IRCA Inform and the ISO 9001 Auditing practises Group in 2009.

A) It is believed that unless Process Audits following an Audit Trail are reintroduced as standard practice there will be no improvement in the credibility of auditing and its ability to ensure the management system is capable of consistently meeting the specified requirements.

B) B) The use of correctly trained Competent personnel knowledgeable in the Product or Service being audited will be critical to ensuring a sustained improvement.

Audit Trail 3.0 BACK TO BASICS

There are many "key" aspects to carrying out professional audits.

There is the need to **audit the process**, defined in ISO 9000 as:—

"**3.4.1 Process** set of interrelated activities which transforms **inputs into outputs**".

It is essential to fully understand the term Process when carrying out an Audit. A process can be demonstrated by

Input—ACTIVITY—Output.

If the process being audited is not understood then it is impossible to do a professional audit.

There is however a critical omission to these defined Terms and Definitions and that is "Audit Trail" it is one of the most important aspects of Auditing yet it is not defined in ISO 9000:2005 It is this link between the two terms that enables the audit to be Professional.

KEY 7:—The failure to carry out a <u>process</u> audit following an <u>audit trail</u> is the single most important reason why audits are not effective

Although applied by some auditors, it is by no means universally accepted. It is this failure to ensure all audits, both internal and external, employ Process audits following an "Audit Trail" that undermines the credibility of audits.

In some cases the need to demonstrate that an audit has been carried out seems to be the objective. The benefit of the audit is compromised and in many cases the audit is a waste of time and effort.

Support for this approach would be strengthened if ISO 9000 had a definition for Audit Trail: Using the standard dictionary definitions for Audit and Trail you can arrive at the following definition.

KEY 8:—AUDIT TRAIL: (Draft as no agreement has been reached action TC 176)

AN EXAMINATION, BY A QUALIFIED PERSON, OF AN ACTIVITY FOLLOWING THE PATH THAT HAS BEEN LEFT BY THE PROCESS

PROCESS

The first thing to be clear about is what is a process?

Following feedback on the Audit Trail article it is clear some people believe the process is the way the procedures are set up and followed during the audit. **This is not true.**

The process is how something is achieved.

The standard identifies a process as:—

INPUT ⟶ ACTIVITY ⟶ OUTPUT

This is a good start, however the term INPUT must include what is required. In other words it needs to specify what the requirements are otherwise it is not possible for the OUTPUT to be checked to see if it meets the Specification.

This specification is the "KEY" to all auditing activity.

If it is not known what is required it is not possible for the auditor to assess the process to see if it is capable of providing a consistent product or service that meets the specification.

The final part of this is the ACTIVITY between the Input and Output and this is what the auditor audits. Professional Auditors will always understand what is required (Specification) for each process they audit and will then, using ISO 9001 clauses evaluate the ACTIVITY to see if it is adequate to consistently meet the specification that is required.

What is an Audit Trail?

As explained in the definition it allows a PATH left by the process to be followed to understand what has taken place. A simple, one off example of this could be that the Organisations purchase order being audited requires a Material Certificate for a bought in item. When the Auditor asks to see this Certificate they can only offer an alternative one as they can't find the one for that particular order. This is of course not acceptable as the TRAIL being followed requires the certificate for the specific order being followed. Even if they had the correct certificate there is more for the auditor to do, how do they control the certificate. How is it received, identified and stored? Does it retain its link to the product it self? If it needs to be passed to the Customer how is this managed? What records are kept? The Audit Trail approach would follow this process through to ensure it is consistently controlled and applied.

Audit Trail 5.0 HOW TO START THE AUDIT

Auditors should always remember why they are conducting the audit. The primary purpose of an audit is to ensure that the process being audited is capable of consistently meeting the specified requirements. It should be noted it is impossible for a 2nd or 3rd Party auditor to carry out a Professional Audit of an Organisation unless the auditor takes the time to understand the specification of the product/service required including any statutory and regulatory requirements. It is this Professional approach to Auditing that allows the auditor to identify the strengths and weaknesses in the process and decide if that Organisation is capable of consistently meeting those specified requirements.

Internal audits should also follow an audit trail, however the audit scope is normally just a small part of the overall process. All of these audits need the auditor to know what the requirements are for the process being audited and should verify that the process with its controls and systems is able to achieve those requirements.

Note: A good approach is to use a form that captures all the names and roles of everyone seen during the audit. It should also identify who attended the opening and closing meeting. (This is useful information when, towards the end of the audit, the training records are checked as this enables personnel from the list to be sampled knowing what they were actually doing during the audit.)

Audit Trail 7.0 PRODUCT REALISATION ISO 9001:2008 section 7.

In order to demonstrate the Audit Trail approach to Process Auditing, sample clauses have been chosen to demonstrate how the audit would be carried out.

Now the sample Contract/s or Order number/s have been identified this is where the audit trail can begin. The biggest mistake auditors make is to think they are only auditing to see if the procedures are being followed. Do not misunderstand what has just been written as procedures, work Instructions, check lists and all the management system are crucial to the ability to achieve customer satisfaction and as such are very important. In fact these together with Competence and Resource Management are the tools that enable Organisations to consistently achieve the specified requirements. The ISO 9001 documented management system, together with the other clauses within the standard are what controls this. The point being made is, as important as they are the purpose of the Audit (section 1.3 of this document) is about whether the Organisation can consistently achieve the requirements of the contract/order placed by the Customer as this is what the auditor is auditing.

Note: The term Contract will now be used for customer order.

Remember there are five main auditing clauses (4-8) within the ISO 9001 standard together with 23 sub clauses. Of these sub clauses 18 may be applicable anywhere within the audit process. To highlight some of these clauses that may be used at any point throughout the Auditing Process they are:—Control of Documents, Control of Records, Responsibility and Authority, Competence and Training, Infrastructure and Work Environment and that's only within Clauses 4 to 6. Clauses should not be audited in isolation.

KEY 9:—ISO 9001 Clauses are NOT what are audited it is the process that is audited.

Does this not highlight that to audit to see if the Management System complies with ISO 9001 is pointless? It is the skill of the auditor to utilise the clauses to ensure all measures are taken to ensure compliance with the specified requirements.

KEY 10:—From above it should be obvious that the purpose of the audit is to ensure that the Management System is adequate to ensure that each process throughout the system is able to consistently achieve and meet the required outputs.

The first step and the one that is so often missing is to understand what the Contract requires. This review of the contract is the "Key" element to Professional auditing.

It requires a detailed look through the relevant documents including drawings, national and international standards and even product standards to select a few important requirements.

The sort of things that should be noted and may come from any part of the contract requirements are for example:—

- Special Hardened Bolts which require Material Certificates and a specific torque
- NP1003 Flame retardant epoxy resin
- Enclosure "O" ring specification
- Gaps between certain PCB contacts
- Depth of blind holes during machining
- Threading tolerances
- Specific tolerances such as +—1% on specific resistors
- Unknown standard called up e.g. EN13980 (Iecex OD/005) Directive 94/9/EC.
- Testing requirements and the certificates provided from this activity
- Marking requirements
- Packing, delivery and preservation requirements
- Declaration of Conformity

Please be aware the above is an example. As you can see it can be anything that is specified. It is not the auditors role to check everything and this is where selective sampling comes in. (Back to Basics No 5 Random Sampling)

There is no simple check list regarding what should be chosen. This is where the auditors eyes and ears pick up and identify anything that would enable them to ensure that the Organisation has identified the requirement and that these have been passed on through the realisation process.

It is this skill of the auditor that enables them to pick out relevant "Key" requirements that will ensure a professional audit.

Where the items chosen are complex with detailed requirements that would take too long to note down, ask for a photocopy of the relevant section or even an uncontrolled copy of a drawing or any other relevant document. This enables you to cross-refer to those documents checking on the specified requirements when going through the process. It is not normally necessary to copy the Objective Evidence seen as your formal note taking is usually sufficient to identify what was seen and whether it was acceptable or not.

The auditor should now have a number of samples that can be used to verify that the process is in control. Other samples can be chosen as the audit progresses.

KEY 11: It is important to remember that selected contract requirements are being audited to see if they have been effectively dealt with and are being met. This is why the auditor must know what the contract says and take a selective sample of those requirements to see if the processes are properly controlled.

KEY 12: It is important throughout the audit to ask each auditee what procedures, instructions, check lists, forms etc they work to and note whether these are the latest version and are Controlled or Uncontrolled documents. (ISO 9001 2008 Ref 4.2.3e) The use of Uncontrolled documents at the point of use are not normally acceptable unless they are used on the day of issue. (You may then wonder why they are uncontrolled)

Note:—Controlled and Uncontrolled Documents are covered in "Back to Basics Guidance Note 11 Controlled Documents.

The planning of the realisation process (7.1)

This is how the Organisation ensures that the processes and systems needed for product realisation are in place. Having chosen the Contract numbers/s of the products that the auditor wishes to follow and seen the contract and what is required the auditor goes to the planning department to see how they have scheduled and passed the instructions to the shop floor. This is where any anomalies or differences to normal should have been identified and passed to the personnel carrying out the next stage. This could include the contract delivery date where a specific time scale has been agreed. Has this been noted and planned into the process? It could be special delivery requirements including documents required etc. The auditor is then able to verify that what has been planned can indeed ensure the product does meet specification. As stated in the ISO 9001 standard, the output of planning shall be in a form suitable for the organisations method of working.

Note:—This is only a sample of this section 7

Audit Trail 9.0 SUMMARY OF SIMPLE AUDIT FLOW

1. Have a walk around the Organisation. Get to understand the layout and see what is taking place at that time. Identify some Contracts/Orders that are actually going through. (Note Contract will be used for customer orders)

2. Go and look at the planning for the products you have taken as your sample and identify how this is handled.

3. Visit the sales department and see what the final agreement was between the Organisation and the Customer for the chosen sampled contracts. Review any modifications and changes that may have been made and ensure that these changes are controlled and agreement obtained between both parties.

4. Review the chosen contracts in detail identifying any specific requirements regarding material to be used, standards and or drawings to be used and any special requirements. Identify the latest issue of all documents. Note the number and issue status of relevant documents such as drawings, material specification against International standards and any odd or special requirements.

5. Find out how the contract requirements are identified and input into the requisition for the material. Go through how this material is purchased and verify that the process does indeed ensure that the purchase order does include all the requirements including Material Certificates, Test Certificates etc that may be necessary to ensure the material ordered is in fact correct.

6. Cover how the goods received are checked to ensure what was ordered was in fact what was delivered. Ensure material received is properly looked after in the stores and how the issue of material to the stores is controlled with reference to relevant material certificates.

7. Identify what instructions and documents control the manufacture of the chosen sampled product. Go through the process ensuring that the process is well controlled and all the called up requirements are adhered to. Identify signed off check

lists, travellers, Route cards etc and any other outputs required e.g. Test Results to see they are complete and the correct authorised persons have signed off the relevant documents.

8. Identify any monitoring and Measuring devices and ensure they are identified with the next due date for calibration. Use the sample taken to verify the records for this activity are properly controlled and correct.

9. Identify how the finished product is approved for release. Who has the authority and what checks and controls apply. It is important to identify what documents need to be sent with the product. Items such as Material Certificates, Test Reports, Operating Instructions, Certificates of Compliance (C of C) and even Declarations of Conformity (D of C). These are just a few of the possible requirements that may be required.

Remember that the objective is to verify that the Management System is capable of ensuring that all the Customer Contracts/Purchase Orders can consistently meet the specified requirements. The above concentrates on the Primary Process and there is of course all the Secondary Processes that support this that needs to be verified throughout the audit.

REMEMBER ISO 9001 2008 IS A TOOL NOT AN OBJECTIVE

To do this the auditor needs to follow the Product realisation process (Sect 7) using the other sections of ISO 9001 to verify that the supporting requirements are adequate to achieve this.

It is this ability to cross-reference the needs of the process against how the sample chosen is controlled and managed that is Key to a Professional Audit.

Audit trail 11.0 BACK TO BASICS GUIDANCE DOCUMENTS

The "Back to Basics" documents were developed over many years of practical experience in order to assist students on the IRCA Auditor Courses. They covered some of the most misunderstood areas of the auditing activities.

WARNING

The documents that follow are not in any special order and do not always have approved formal definitions where they do they are identified. It should be recognised that in running training courses it is important to explain how each of the terms below may be used.

Each of these "Back to Basics" documents are written as "Stand Alone" documents so there is some repetition within these documents.

As shown in the case of "Audit Trail" there is no definition and that is why it is only a suggested definition. Also D of C and C of C have different interpretation but are becoming used more often and could do with a common ISO definition as even C of C has different wording depending on who is using it.

GUIDANCE DOCUMENTS

1. **Audit Trail**
2. Objective Evidence
3. **Specification**
4. Audit Criteria
5. **Random Sample**
6. Audit Findings
7. **Audit Evidence**
8. Competence
9. **Declaration Of Conformity (D of C)**

10. Certificates of Compliance (C of C)
11. **Controlled Documents**
12. Certification

It is recognised that not all personnel may accept all the comments in each Guidance Note but hopefully it may start a discussion that will resolve any issue of concern. e.g. Audit Trail

The author would be pleased to receive any constructive comments both positive and negative in order to improve these guidance notes.

Audit Trail Part 1 Audit Trail

Audit trail is one of the most important aspects of Auditing. If you don't follow an audit trail the most you can check is whether the individual documents you look at are correctly filled in.

Dictionary Definitions

Audit

An Examination by qualified persons of, accounts of a business, public office or **an undertaking.**

Normally related to Financial Activities but latterly used by Quality Practioner's to assess the ability of an Organisation to comply with specified requirements.

Trail

Part drawn behind or in the wake of a thing

Track left by thing that has been moved or been drawn over a surface.

Track, scent or **beaten path.**

Lets link these together and we have:—

Audit Trail

An examination, by a qualified person, of an activity. Following the path that has been left by the process.

So what does this mean?

Lets take a simple purchasing activity

How is the decision to purchase made? Who decides what is required and do they have the authority? How is this advised to the supplier? Who chooses the supplier and by what criteria? How is the specification decided? Is it adequate?

- It is essential that you take your sample/s (This is your starting point)
- Then use the sample/s to identify the process taken such as:—
  - o What drove the process e.g. what controls the process, how are decisions made.
  - o Who has the authority
  - o Who decides quantities
  - o Who decides specification
  - o How is specification controlled

The most important thing is to ensure that the samples are LINKED that they are from the same TRAIL.

If you are following the trail of a HORSE there is no point ending up trailing a DONKEY.

Note:—this is the original document issued in 2006 after ISO 9000 2005 had been issued

Audit Trail Part 3 Specification

The term **"Specification"** (3.7.3) is defined in ISO 9000 2005 as:—

Document stating requirements.

It is impossible to carry out a Professional Audit if you have not looked at the **document stating requirements** for any process you may be asked to audit.

Lets also look at **Audit (3.9.1)**

Systematic, independent and documented process for obtaining audit evidence and evaluating it objectively to determine the extent to which audit criteria are fulfilled.

We will come to **audit criteria** later in the guidance documents however one audit criteria for ISO 9001 audits is, of course, the ISO 9001 2008 standard itself. There are people who believe they are there to Audit to see if "the system complies with ISO 9001 2008!!"

However they forget then to look at the standard itself that clearly states within the Scope:—

1.1   General section

This International Standard specifies requirements for a quality management system where an organisation:—
   needs to demonstrate its ability to consistently provide a product that meets customer and applicable regulatory requirements.

The purpose of the audit is to see if the Management System is able to control the process in a manner that can ensure the product or service can consistently be met. The method of doing this is by judging the process used against the clauses within the ISO 9001 standard to verify that the system can achieve this.

Which then leads us back to **specification.**

The document stating requirements is usually the Purchase order or contract received from their customer. It is sometimes difficult for new auditors to understand that the term purchase order is used both for Customers Purchase Orders and the Organisation own Purchase Orders used to obtain material from their suppliers. For simplicity, in this article, **we will refer to customer requirements as the "Contract"**.

The simplest form of contract is when the Organisation is making a product to its own specification. The process then is to look at the specification identifying any special requirements or standards that are called up and going through Section 7 of ISO 9001 2008 (Product Realisation) to ensure all the specifications are being controlled throughout the process. The more difficult type of contract is where the Customer specifies what is required as this then brings in more interfaces over the product and what is required.

Both Contracts will take the form of checking National and International standards within the contract as well as any other specifications including drawings. (if applicable). As the sample has already been chosen only requirements that relate to that particular product or service are examined. This is part of the sampling process.

A professional auditor will always be looking for some critical requirement. It may be a special material, tolerance or clearance or an unusual standard that is called up. From this sample he will have identified a number of specific materials that needs to be purchased and from this the controls that need to be in place to meet the specified requirements.

This in turn leads to the purchasing department, where the requisitions or standard buying descriptions can be examined within the Organisation, to again understand the specification and check that all requirements are covered in the Purchase Order to the supplier.

The process then continues to the receipt of the material and what checks, material certificates, certificates of conformity, declarations of conformity are required to verify the material is acceptable. It may even cover acceptance criteria.

It is not the intention in this guidance note to go through the whole Product Realisation process, but to give an idea of what should take place re verifying that the process does demonstrate the ability to consistently provide a product that meets customer and applicable regulatory requirement

This failure to comply with ISO 9001 2008 1.1 General Section **needs to demonstrate its ability to consistently provide a product that meets customer and applicable regulatory requirements.**

This is why audits have, in some areas, lost their credibility in the market place.

Audit Trail Part 5 Random Sample

The term "Random Sample" is regularly used by Auditors.

It is often understood to mean where the auditor takes a sample completely at random.

This is incorrect if you wish to do professional audits.

Another term currently being used is "Selective or Representative Sample" which can be interpreted as an "**Intelligent** selection of **relevant** samples".

So what do we mean by this.

Professional auditors will look at the process being audited. What does the company make or do.

Secondly what is relevant to why you are auditing.

Finally look at what a company has been making recently.

A good thing to do is try to do a walk around at the beginning of the audit to see what is currently taking place.

In the case of a product being made what is on the shop floor.

In the case of a service what is being actioned at present.

Lets take an example of a 2nd party audit. The auditor/s will look at what product or service their organisation wishes to purchase. This enables them to look for similar products that are or have been produced for another company. The auditors will then look at this sample and select a relevant Contract or Purchase Order.

One item is not a sample. So the auditor may take one or two of the above directly related jobs and then one or two others totally at random to see how robust their system is.

This mainly depends on the time allowed. A 2nd Party Audit particularly if it is a large contract may only have time to sample just one to three contracts and not necessarily go through the whole process for all of them.

Where it is a simple process the auditor may sample 20 or more.

The sample chosen is, from the auditor's point of view, a way of checking by sample that the process is working. In doing this, the auditor wants to feel comfortable that the sample taken will give confidence that the system is working effectively.

Whether you take three or twenty plus is a decision for the auditor.

Lets take an example of a Hospital. You look at what is being purchased and take a random sample of 5 things. They turn out to be Paper Clips, Plastic waste bags, A4 paper, Ink jet cartridges and Light Bulbs.

Is your audit going to Add useful information regarding the primary process within the hospital? Is your audit value adding?

Please do not misunderstand, it is important to have general items within the audit however we are back to the original statement the selection should be **Intelligent** and **Relevant** and that the auditor should feel the sample chosen gives confidence that the system is working and will allow the organisation to produce products or services that meet the customers needs.

Audit evidence is the documented records you see or the information you obtain which can be compared with the audit criteria.

Audit Trail Part 7 Audit Evidence

Audit evidence is the documented records you see or the information you obtain which can be compared with the audit criteria.

ISO 9000: 2005 section 3.9.4 Audit Evidence

Records (3.7.6) statements of fact or other **information (3.7.1) that,** are relevant to the **audit criteria (3.9.3)** and verifiable.

If for example a procedure stated that all Purchase Orders should be reviewed and signed off by the senior Buyer. Then during the audit you notice that out of the 5 Purchase Orders you had seen, only three had been signed off by the senior Buyer. The Buyer who had produced these orders had signed the other two him self. You would then make a note of which orders you actually looked at. You are then able to raise this against the audit criteria and include the relevant procedure or the ISO 9001 2008 standard and clause as appropriate. The Purchase Order numbers are the Objective Evidence. e.g P.O 13679, 14320 (See Objective Evidence)

Audit evidence could also be where you check for a form that should be used and find that it is no longer used. This is audit evidence in the way of information but would not be Objective Evidence because you cannot go back and see this particular form as it does not exist.

It can also be where you check the stock items and all items are in the correct locations and are in good condition and stored in a careful practical manner. You should always write down the items you actually looked at. e.g The 2 inch cast Iron valves in box E23, The 0-50 bar pressure gauges in box F 19 and the 6" Ring Type Gaskets in box E 29 were all in the correct location etc. (This is good positive reporting as this was correct)

In simple terms the Audit Evidence is all the information both good and bad that you write down onto your Audit Checklist or Findings. It may be Objective Evidence or something that is missing and not seen or even something you are told. Where you are only told something is not done as required by the procedure, you should check it out and get confirmation from the parties involved before writing it onto your Checklist.

Audit Evidence should cover both the **GOOD** things that are found as well as the things that do not comply or make sense.

It is from this Audit Evidence that you will develop the Audit Findings that are presented to the Auditee and their Management at the closing meeting. It is good audit practice to comment on the good things that are found. When you report your findings you should be comfortable in reporting where processes were seen to be working well. E.g. If the stores area was seen to be well controlled this should be mentioned during the closing meeting. When this is done the auditee is never normally asked to show the evidence, however, the auditor should be able to present the evidence that has been found that allows the auditor to make that statement. It should never be "I think its good"," or "it appears to be working well". It either was it was not. Always remember to advise the auditee that the audit only covers a sample and that this does not mean there are no problems anywhere else.

Audit Trail Part 9 Declaration of Conformity (D of C)

Dictionary Definition:—

"Declaration" (n) Stating and announcing, openly and explicitly, or formally; emphatic, solemn or legal assertion or proclamation.

"Conformity" (n) Compliance with "Liable" (adj) legally bound answerable for

Declaration of Conformity n

A legal assertion that the item provided is in compliance with the specification.

The Declaration of Conformity is one of the common threads throughout the CE marking directives.

There is a need in certain industries to provide a Declaration of Conformity for every product that is made.

This is certainly true when Organisations provide equipment that is used in Explosive Atmospheres. (ATEX). The Declaration of Conformity may be used in many different industries where it is important to verify what the product complies with.

What does this mean?

In simple terms it is to ensure that each individual product produced has a certificate signed by a responsible person in the Organisation to confirm that the actual product they have provided does comply with the specifications called up.

So what is the difference between this and the Order or Contract Requirements?

It is really to identify one individual within the supplying Organisation who is legally responsible for that product complying with the specification.

There is a misconception by senior personnel that when they sign this they are only signing to say the product is verified and validated to be able to meet its approved design requirements. This unfortunately is not true. They are signing to say that particular product made that day has been made to the approved specification. They are therefore liable should this product, for whatever reason, not meet the specified requirements in compliance with the approval given for that product.

When this is explained the first reaction is "Well I am not signing it as I don't actually make it myself". This is where a management system that is in compliance with ISO 9001 should, if applied correctly, give all the information necessary to ensure that each product does in fact comply. There are normally "Route Cards", "Check Lists", "Test Results", etc that if completed properly and traceable to the individual contract or batch number ensure that the product does comply. If the process for signing and issuing the D of C is only done when all the relevant activities within the process have been signed by the relevant Competent Personnel at each stage of the process, then, and only then, can a D of C be issued to go with the product. Obviously the person issuing the D of C must have checked that all the relevant documents have been completed and signed off by the competent personnel. The person issuing the D of C may or may not be the person who has signed the D of C. It is, however, the responsible party who verifies that all requirements have been met who is ultimately responsible but as long as each process has been signed off to be in compliance that should ensure that the responsibility is on each and every person in the process.

Audit Trail Part 11 Controlled Documents

What is meant by Controlled Documents?

There are two types of document in use in Quality management systems and they are "Controlled" and "Uncontrolled" Documents.

There can be a lot of confusion about what this means especially now that there are complete quality management systems all controlled on computer.

It is worth going back over the intention of having Controlled Documents when the system was just a "Hard Copy" paper system.

The ISO 9001 standard is quite specific in section 4.2.3e Control of Documents where it states controls needed to ensure that relevant versions of the applicable documents are available at point of use. This is quite easy to understand, as it is a sensible approach that allows personnel to work with the latest version of any documents. These documents are not just procedural documents but can be Drawings, Quality Plans, National and International Standards or any other document that is needed by the individual to do their job.

There have been many examples where if a copy is taken off the computer the copy is automatically identified as "Uncontrolled" only valid on day of print.

This approach is sometimes used as a method of ensuring that the system cannot be blamed if personnel use uncontrolled copies, however this is not the way to run a QMS. The QMS is supposed to work for the user not the user work for the system.

Going back to 4.2.3e above the intention of the standard is to ensure that the system controls the issue of the procedures and other QMS documents in a manner that all personnel have, at the point of use, access to the latest version of any documents they need to do their job. It is not acceptable to issue Uncontrolled Documents to personnel who need these documents on a day to day basis unless it is used that day: e.g. a check list that is filled in at that time. If it is a procedure then this should certainly be issue controlled to those without a computer.

This use of "Uncontrolled" documents is an area that is prone to error. If personnel have printed "Uncontrolled" QMS documents off the computer and use them because they need to refer to a Hard Copy version to do their job, then those copies should be hard copy "Controlled" documents. The suggestion that it is the users responsibility to check the issue status defeats the purpose of the QMS. The system is there to ensure that each individual has the latest versions in a format that enables them to do their work.

So what does Controlled documents mean?

In simple terms it means you do not have to check the documents yourself to see if the version is the latest as the system will, when a new updated document is issued, ensure you are aware of or sent a new "Controlled" copy of the document. Then you are either asked to destroy or return the old copy dependent on what your procedure for Control of Document states.

You can normally, in a properly controlled system, be sure that the version you have access to on the computer is the latest version. It is unacceptable for the system to demand that the user has to confirm whether they are working to the latest version, as the system should do this.

Uncontrolled Documents

Users of uncontrolled documents know they will not be advised of any revision.

There have been many instances where personnel who do not have a computer are issued with Uncontrolled copies. This is wrong and unacceptable as uncontrolled documents are documents issued for information only.

Audit Trail 13.0 AUTHORS APOLOGY

Finally, the author would like to apologise to all Professional Auditors who see this as a pointless document because they already carry out Audits in this manner.

This document only asks users to understand that the intention is to give all auditors the opportunity to improve and possibly do better Professional Audits to the benefit of the Auditee and the Purchasers who need reliable information about Organisations.

Over many decades of carrying out audits various auditing mistakes have been made some of which are relayed to students during Audit Training Courses so that new auditors may learn from these mistakes thereby avoiding making errors of their own. This in turn can then improve the Quality of auditing to the benefit of all parties.

If you have any suggestions for improving this document please contact David Seear by email. **daveseear@btinternet.com**

FINAL Thoughts

1. Do you wish to have some input into the definition for "Audit Trail"? As you will have seen throughout this document the failure to follow an Audit Trail could be the single most important reason why audits are not effective. PDQ Management Services would ask readers to send in their definitions to daveseear@ btinternet.com. Become part of the solution not the problem.
2. The reason this document was developed was because the author was encouraged to put together a guidance document for auditing following articles on "Audit Trail".

This has now developed into a 3 to 5 year improvement project see (Appendix C)

It would be naive to expect Certification Bodies to accept a step change to auditing however if UKAS and other accreditation bodies insisted that at least one audit, of the three annual audits that take place up to the tri-annual visit, should be solely a product/service audit this should not, for professional Certification Bodies, cause a problem.

Unless all Certification bodies and in particular Accreditation bodies buy into this there is no chance of improving Certification Auditing. It is now a competitive business and although the old AMDAC table could bring some realistic "Man Days" to auditing it is not always being used. Even with realistic man-days unless the audits are process audits following an audit trail to verify the specifications are being met they will be ineffectual. In fact any Certification Body and even Accreditation Body going it alone would soon be out of business.

Audit Trail Appendix A

KEY LISTING

KEY 1: REMEMBER ISO 9001 IS THE TOOL NOT THE OBJECTIVE

KEY 2:—All audits should give the audited Organisation information about how robust their systems are in ensuring that they can consistently meet the required specification.

KEY 3:—It has been accepted that some Purchasing Organisations have reduced confidence in ISO 9001 Certification.

KEY 4:—The Statutory and Regulatory requirements called up in ISO 9001 clause 1.1a) are only those requirements that relate to the product/service itself.

KEY 5:—There is still a belief that that Audits are to see if the ISO 9001 Certification clauses are covered within the Organisations Management System. This is incorrect as it conveys little or no information on how effective the processes are.

KEY 6:—From the above it is obvious that all auditing is about ensuring that the organisation can consistently meet the specified requirements.

KEY 7:—The failure to carry out a <u>process </u>audit following an <u>audit trail</u> is the single most important reason why audits are not effective

KEY 8:—AUDIT TRAIL: (Draft as no agreement has been reached action)

AN EXAMINATION, BY A QUALIFIED PERSON, OF AN ACTIVITY FOLLOWING THE PATH THAT HAS BEEN LEFT BY THE PROCESS

KEY 9:—ISO 9001 Clauses are <u>NOT</u> what are audited it is the process that is audited.

KEY 10:—From above it should be obvious that the purpose of the audit is to ensure that the Management System is adequate to ensure that each process throughout the system is able to consistently achieve and meet the required outputs.

KEY 11: It is important to remember that selected contract requirements are being audited to see if they have been effectively dealt with and are being met. This is why the auditor must know what the contract says and take a selective sample of those requirements to see if the processes are properly controlled.

KEY 12: It is important throughout the audit to ask each auditee what procedures, instructions, check lists, forms etc they work to and note whether these are the latest version and are Controlled or Uncontrolled documents. (ISO 9001 2008 Ref 4.2.3e) The use of Uncontrolled documents at the point of use are not normally acceptable unless they are used on the day of issue. (You may then wonder why they are uncontrolled)

KEY 13: It is important that having identified National or International standards that are called up in the Contract that the method of ensuring they are working to the latest version is effective. Does the contract identify the applicable version? Does the system in place have access to the latest issues?

KEY 14:—ISO 9001 requires that only the applicable elements of the standard that are required to ensure your product can consistently meet the specified requirements need be addressed. (Other than Mandatory requirements)

KEY 15:—It is vital the auditor understands the requirements of the requisition and ensures these requirements match the specification from the contract.

KEY 16:—It is at this point that it is important to remind auditors how important it is to gather audit evidence (ISO 9000 3.9.4) of what was seen. (Guidance Note Part 7)

KEY 17:—Always follow the chosen Audit Trail as it is too easy for auditors to take samples at different stages of the process that are not related or linked to the sample/s chosen. This leads to the auditor only being able to check if a document is filled in correctly, missing out on being able to verify that the process is actually working.

KEY 18:—The importance of starting manufacture with the correct grade and specification for the material is paramount as using the wrong material in production would ensure the Product did not meet specification. It should be noted any change in material must have customer approval. Use of the so called 'better' grade of material without design change justification and approval is not acceptable.

KEY 19 Auditing of the manufacturing process would entail physically reviewing the items in production and sampling any dimensional requirements such as "Blind Hole" depths in castings etc. Auditing is not just a paper exercise.

KEY 20:—Auditing of a process must follow an audit trail or it is impossible to verify that requirements are being met.

KEY 21:—The important issue is to follow the same item throughout the activity to verify that the process is in fact controlled and would ensure the specification was achieved each time.

KEY 22:—In the closing meeting you would always advise the Organisation that you have audited by sampling and that because you have not identified anything wrong it does not mean there is nothing wrong.

KEY 23:—Some auditors spend more time ensuring each element of the ISO 9001 Standard has a "Tick" against it than ensuring the system is effective.

KEY 24:—Professional Auditing is NOT about seeing if the management system complies with ISO 9001 but seeing that the system used within that Organisation is capable of consistently meeting the specified contract requirements.

This can only be done if you follow an Audit Trail.

This book is the second book published by the author. It is dedicated to improving the knowledge of the four standards in the ISO 9000 Family of Standards. The first book "ISO 9001 Audit Trail" was first published in March 2010. This new book compliments the other by taking a broader view of the purpose of the ISO 9000 Family of standards. It is recognised that the standard of ISO 9001 auditing is mixed and in some cases poor. The Audit Trail book was developed following a request to produce a practical guide to auditing following the publication of "Understanding the Audit Trail" published by IRCA Inform Issue 24 on the 10ᵗʰ December 2009.

http://www.irca.org/inform/issue24/Seear.html

A similar article is also in
www.iso.org/tc176/ISO9001AuditingPracticesGroup

In highlighting the ISO 9000 Family of Standards and the roles that each standard plays within that Family. The intention is that the purpose and scope of each standard will be better understood and some of the confusion will be removed. It has been decided that as the "ISO 9001 Audit Trail" book is relevant, extracts from the 1ˢᵗ edition have been included as appendix F.

This document is for Organisations that use any of the four ISO 9000 Family of Standards and those who are auditors or carry out auditor training. It has been developed from the Original Back to Basics guidance documents used during auditor training. (Sample Attached.) The attached guidance notes within the Back to Basics may be used as individual training notes to help Organisations improve.

About the Author

David John Seear C.Eng CMarEng FIMarEST FCQI CQP is a Chartered Engineer who spent 12 years at sea ending up as Chief Engineer with a combined First Class Chief Engineers certificate before leaving and joining Shell. He left Shell U.K after 20 years service where he had been Head Of Quality and Performance for Shell UK Materials. One of the departments reporting to him was Quality Appraisal whose purpose was to carry out 2nd party audits for Shell UK and Shell den Hague. He represented the CBI on BSI QMS 22 for 6 years and represented the U.K. on ISO 9000 TC 176 for 3 years.

He has lived in Brunei and Abu Dhabi and carried out Audits and/or Training throughout the world including Africa, North and South America, Russia as well as the areas lived in namely the Far East and Middle East,

He is an IRCA Principal Auditor of 25 years experience and runs PDQ Management Services that carries out Training, Auditing, Consultancy and Lecturing on various management issues including procurement and management Systems. email daveseear@ btinternet.com

www.ingramcontent.com/pod-product-compliance
Lightning Source LLC
Chambersburg PA
CBHW051413280526
45785CB00003B/1057